ETHIOPIA
INCORPORATED

Transforming the Way Businesses Run in Africa

MERIED BEKELE

ISBN: 978-1-956464-55-9

First Edition 2024

Published by BrightRay Publishing
https://brightray.com/

PRAISE FOR
ETHIOPIA
INCORPORATED

Ethiopia Incorporated shows the opportunity for entrepreneurship in Africa, especially in Ethiopia. By including personal stories and experiences, Meried provides a multi-faceted analysis of the challenges and opportunities in our country, suggesting practical solutions through an effective structure. The profound message not only inspires young professionals but also raises awareness and teaches. It is positively impactful."

—Dr. Ahmedin Mohammed,
Former State Minister of MinT
and the Ministry of Defence

Ethiopia Incorporated flashed me back to some of my memories at MinT, Ethio Telecom, and all the stories I used to hear so much about. It reminded me of the good old days, full of challenges and opportunities. Meried's reflections are unique and educational, and he does an amazing job of combining his thoughts and life story with business principles."

—Amare Herpie,
CIO of Commercial Bank of Ethiopia
and Former COO of Ethio Telecom

I recommend *Ethiopia Incorporated* to young Ethiopian entrepreneurs, business professionals, and policymakers interested in economic development. Its combination of personal narrative and practical advice makes it a powerful tool for those looking to make a difference in Ethiopia's business landscape."

—Biniam G. Hiwet,
Founder and Managing Director
of Avicom Trading PLC

Meried's story is truly inspiring. Even though I was fortunate to know him well during his college years, reading about his journey was still a captivating experience. Most importantly, his humility is a signature of his success."

—Dr. Yohannes Alemseged,
Former Mekelle University Professor

Ethiopia Incorporated is unapologetically honest and brave. Meried does a marvelous job of compacting a grossly complicated topic, particularly in the context of Ethiopia. His personal stories makes the book readable and relatable. I am sure it will go a long way in helping the youth of our country."

—Tibebeselassie A. Tedla,
Founder and CEO of Timex Trading PLC

Ethiopia Incorporated delivers an insightful and inspiring exploration of the evolving persona of Meried Bekele from a humble beginning to an established entrepreneur. Meried's engaging writing style manages to link how social, cultural, religious, and political issues crafted the Ethiopian mindset in all aspects of life, making complex business practices and concepts friendly without diluting their significance. This skillful writing ensures that the book is not only informative but also a pleasure to read."

**—Anteneh Awoke,
IT Systems Coordinator at
the African Union**

Ethiopia Incorporated provides equal motivation for seasoned professionals and would-be entrepreneurs. It is a blessing to share one's experience and knowledge as a way to give back."

**—Debbol Shenkute,
Blockchain Solutions Architect at
Input Output**

*To the young African entrepreneurs
and professionals
fighting to solve problems:*

Your ambitions are possible.

TABLE OF
CONTENTS

EVERY CHALLENGE BRINGS
OPPORTUNITY

In 2007, the tallest building in Ethiopia had 12 floors. My hotel room in Tokyo, within walking distance from the Cisco office where I would take my CCIE exam, sat on the 36th floor, not even the highest part of the building.

I arrived in Japan one day before the exam, meaning I had 24 hours to recover from jetlag. I took the day to walk around, take in a brief experience of Japanese culture, and relax my nerves in preparation for the long, intensive assessment. The next day, I woke up and walked to the examination site. For eight and a half hours, with only one 30-minute break, fewer than 10 other test participants and I sat and completed the practical exam, proving we could build a global network connecting San Francisco, New York, London, and Tokyo. The test administrators provided physical devices that we had to wire with the aim of building a functional product. To do so within the time restriction, we had to have enough experience to operate with both speed and accuracy, as if we had done it a hundred times before. Going in for the first time, the expectation was that we would fail twice before finally earning the certification—that is, if we were lucky. On average, even senior network engineers with 10 years of experience typically took three tries to pass the exam. With five minutes remaining on the clock, I finished the last test question and submitted my answers.

The Cisco examiners took another day to analyze and report each participant's test results. As I waited to hear news of my score, I walked around Tokyo for the short time I had left in the city. The cultural differences between it and Addis Ababa, my hometown, were apparent. In Ethiopia, we are relaxed—we do not walk so fast. But in Japan, thousands of people hurried down the streets and sidewalks, crossing the roads at traffic lights and moving in and out of skyscrapers and shops. I felt overwhelmed but excited. Here was a country that knew industry and opportunity, all without sacrificing its culture or traditions. The structural and federal support for businesses of all kinds, for entrepreneurs of all kinds, showed me the extensive importance of economic competency for a country's livelihood and its people.

Then, I received word from the examiners: At age 24, I passed the exam on my first try, becoming the only person in Ethiopia with a CCIE certificate.

When I returned home, the director of the government institution where I worked looked surprised.

"You came back?" he asked. "You were only there for three days, and you came back?"

"Yes," I responded. "I only went for the exam. I had nothing else to do there."

I touched a computer for the first time as a second-year college student attending Mekelle University in the capital of Tigray, which is 780 kilometers north of Addis Ababa. As a part of the first electrical engineering class offered at the university, my interest in technology continued to grow and expand as time went on and as opportunities presented themselves. By my third year, our department head guided us to establish a student technology club called State of the Art (SOTA) in an effort to learn more about website and software development, which interested me more than the electrical part of my major. I served as the first president of SOTA.

In 2001, the university only had one computer lab, complete with dial-up internet. Every student, no matter the major, used the same handful of computers to check Yahoo Mail or American Online, later named AOL. With no broadband internet, a single Google search could take a full minute or two to show results, making any project research a hair-pulling task. Finding and combing through a library book almost proved to be a quicker way of finding information.

However, despite the obvious limitations, I recognized the potential of automation, digitization, and information sharing. Even then, the profound impact of technology was not lost on me. That is why, when the department head approached SOTA and requested we build the university's website from scratch as part of a summer internship program, I gave an immediate yes. The university did not even have the beginnings of a website to detail course descriptions, enrollment information, or faculty listings. The entire project, from purchasing a domain name to coding the layout, would be our responsibility, all without the easy-to-use website builders now available in the modern day. From that moment on, my interest in computers was ignited— so much so that by the time other students returned from summer break, the website was up and running: functional, easy to navigate, and fully compliant with the university's branding.

In my fourth year of college, a leading IT company approached SOTA with yet another summer internship opportunity, particularly for the four students who contributed to the website. The company intended to build the campus's network and the university's data center, and it wished to select certain students to assist with the initiative.

While helping build the network and learning quite a bit, I was also introduced to Cisco, an American network company based in San Francisco. More interestingly, I learned about Cisco's global certification programs, some of the most prestigious in the world. Those at the IT company warned me against taking the CCNA test, an entry-level IT certification that covers networking fundamentals, too early. To pass, I would need to study for at least a year or have more prior experience. But seeing as I had three months before my internship ended, I said to myself, "Let me buy some books and read about it."

During the same internship, I studied, went to the exam center, and passed the two-hour exam, effectively earning my CCNA certification. When I returned for my fifth and final year of university, I was the only one with the credential and likely the only person, student or professor, to earn it in the school's history. My immediate thought was to pass the knowledge on to others and share what I learned from my studies. During lunchtime, I began hosting one-hour lectures on networking for any interested students. My instructor even sat in on these lectures and watched as no one else in the university could speak about networking from the CCNA level. Without yet earning a bachelor's degree, I felt as if I had made an impact on the people around me. Inspired and driven, I continued forward.

Post-graduation, the leading IT company where I carried out an internship offered me a full-time position as a network engineer. I worked with international experts and senior-level Ethiopians, all of whom saw my energy and passion for the work and would offload tasks onto me as a result. Happy to take the work they handed me, I would deliver projects, work anywhere from 80 to 100 hours per week, and learn more than

I thought possible. The speed at which I turned in projects boosted my confidence—to the point where I started asking, "Why don't I take the expert-level exam?"

As of 2024, Cisco certifications are likened to the PhDs of the IT industry, having certified more than four million people and now administering numerous certifications across four defined levels of expertise. But in the early 2000s, Cisco only offered three levels of certification: entry (CCNA), professional (CCNP), and expert (CCIE). If you had the experience and could pass the exam, you did not have to earn your CCNP to pursue a CCIE. From my research, I learned that CCIE experts, on average, made $150,000 to $200,000 annual salaries, and by passing the exam, those with the certification could apply and work for just about any prestigious company of their choice. As a young man in my early 20s, I wanted nothing more than to move to the US and be a distinguished engineer in Silicon Valley, and the CCIE appeared as a pathway to that goal . . . except for three obstacles that stood in the way:

1. No one in the entire nation of Ethiopia had the certification.

2. Only 10 places in the world offered the test, none of which were on the continent of Africa, and obtaining a visa would prove incredibly difficult.

3. The company I worked for would not sponsor the expensive test and trip abroad, given that I had only been employed there for a year.

I remained ambitious and, despite the setbacks, found a way. As I looked for alternate routes, a friend introduced me to a government role that had a built-in budget for employee training. Unfortunately, the career change meant a decrease in my salary, but I saw this move as an investment in my future.

Applying for the position required maneuvering through bureaucratic barriers and a written exam, but I passed as the top scorer and was promptly hired as a technical engineer to manage the government's network data center, WoredaNet. Hosted in the prime minister's office, the data center was used to conduct video conference meetings with other federal and state officials across the country. Over the next few months, I stayed late at the office, as I had done at my previous job, and provided coaching to more senior employees. Often remaining at work until 10 or 11 p.m., the prime minister's secret service would occasionally knock on the door and ask, "What are you doing? You have to go home!"

My reputation slowly grew until I became known as "that engineer who fixes problems and works hard." The prestigious position I was in, combined with my known character, enabled me to apply for a portion of the training budget, which was then granted to me the next year. I then started preparing for the CCIE.

At the time I scheduled my test, only a few places in the US and Europe still had openings, but a long queue prohibited me from signing up. The only place that allowed me to book a spot was Tokyo, Japan. Though I looked forward to the opportunity, having never been out of the country, I also realized how strenuous the process of obtaining a visa would be. As someone from Ethiopia, the government would not want me to leave Africa, thinking that, like most, I would never return.

I first tried to apply for a visa so I could attend preparatory training in London before the CCIE exam, but the visa officer at the UK embassy rejected the application: "You must be kidding. You want to go to London less than two years after graduating? No way."

But then, with the director of the government institution backing me with a strong support letter, I applied once more and finally received the visa, though another officer warned me again and again, "When you return from the UK, you *must* report back to the embassy. You *must*."

"Of course, of course," I reassured.

I flew to London, completed the training, flew back home, and reported to the embassy. I had no interest in staying a day more than necessary. I had my eyes set on higher ambitions.

The definition of luck I love most is "when preparation meets opportunity."[1] To study for the test, I fully committed. Taking a four-month leave from work, my life revolved around practice materials, textbooks, mock labs, and virtual machinery. I even left my family's home and rented an apartment on my own, needing a place to myself so I could focus. I had no high priorities in my life, other than passing the CCIE exam.

Months later, I embarked on a long, 24-hour trip from airport to airport and finally landed in Tokyo where, as you know, my studying paid off and I passed.

The backbone of my inspiration lies in commitment. I believe in giving back to those who propelled me forward. For example, I knew that I could have repaid the cost of the CCIE exam in a few months had I taken an international job with, say, Microsoft or Cisco as I once planned. However, the government sponsored my training and travels—to repay Ethiopia, I had to stay, work, and contribute, all while growing my skills and developing my profession. Because I had the time, expertise, and energy, I could not simply abandon the country that gave me a chance.

In the same vein, I had to repay my parents, who encouraged my education from a young age. My parents never finished high school, and growing up, I remember them working low-income jobs: serving at restaurants, completing administrative work, and cleaning hotels, among other professions. The way out of the cycle, they found, was sending their children to school and promoting their learning. As the eldest son, I worked for As and remained in the top-scoring percentiles from kindergarten to high school. Having seen my identity form around my academic performance, my parents bought me books whenever possible, which I would read countless times. Again and again, I heard, "Oh, he will become a doctor! He will become an engineer!" Those early aspirations shaped my future and gave me the confidence to strive for more.

Nearly two decades later, less than 10 CCIEs have come from Ethiopia, and even fewer continue living in the country. Global markets require high levels of expertise, meaning large corporations will offer technology experts high-paying salaries and even arrange for them and their families to move to America or Europe. Most professionals, from all industries, will accept these offers, not seeing a way to progress in their home country. I can understand doing so, especially when many people want better lives for their children, for Ethiopia presents many challenges: war, poverty, food insecurity, educational system flaws, healthcare inaccessibility, technology outages, and economic strife. However, the way I view my home as an entrepreneur is this: Every challenge brings opportunity.

I have been very fortunate to drive impact in a developing country. My company, IE Network Solutions, was not born out of a risk-taking, entrepreneurial attitude. Rather, I describe myself as an "accidental entrepreneur," someone who initially established a business to account for freelance work but then identified and maximized value from a significant market gap. Since its establishment in 2008, IE Networks has strived to be Ethiopia's leading IT company, and despite the opportunities abroad, it is still located and operated in Addis Ababa. Over the years, IE Networks has worked as the nation's main enterprise solutions provider, amassed more than 200 employees, and collaborated with major global brands, including Mastercard, Visa, H&M, and General Electric, and notable Ethiopian services, including Ethiopian Airlines and the Commercial Bank of Ethiopia. For our next step, we aim to inspire industry-forward change in our community by educating future African business leaders and helping government agencies resolve economic, federal, and social issues via legislative power. Through systemized innovation, Ethiopia can become an industry-empowered country that generates substantial internal revenue through business development, foreign investment, and international involvement, such as outsourcing practices.

IE Networks prioritizes KPIs, a strong work ethic, and an efficient project management process—a mimicable blueprint that can be adopted by businesses across the continent. Startups and small businesses are the lifeblood of any economy. More commerce and employment means individuals can acquire a steady income to support their families, the government can benefit from generating more internal revenue, and banks can increase their offerings to both profit and distribute more opportunities to these business owners. Multiply this out, and true change will take place.

Seventeen years after taking the CCIE exam, my dream is no longer to find an opportunity outside the country. All that I have built here—IE Networks, my reputation, the livelihoods of my employees—is worth preserving.

So what is my dream now?

To be the living proof that building a successful, private business in Ethiopia is not only possible but gratifying.

An engineer by trade, I know that the core of most problems is *not understanding the problem itself.* To eliminate any uncertainty or confusion around certain obstacles, this book adopts a problem-solution structure. From historic, economic, and scientific standpoints, each chapter defines and analyzes a major challenge Ethiopian entrepreneurs face and then outlines potential solutions, exemplified by personal anecdotes from more than 16 years of building, developing, and refining IE Networks. And though one book cannot solve the highly complex issue of Ethiopian economic development, this book simply attempts to find pathways for promoting entrepreneurship within the country. Rather than one specific, defined solution, it encourages creativity and innovative thinking. It provides possibilities.

CHAPTER OUTLINE

➤ Chapter One: **Accidental Entrepreneur**

- This chapter tells the origin story of IE Networks. I did not establish the IT company because I hoped to scale it into a national enterprise. Rather, IE Networks was originally used to manage my part-time freelance work and grew from there, making me an "accidental entrepreneur."

➤ Chapter Two: **Beyond Just Enough**

- **Problem:** Several sectors in Ethiopia are vital to society yet inefficient, including education, healthcare, infrastructure, and agriculture.

- **Solution:** Entrepreneurship is the only true solution, yet many challenges deter aspiring business owners.

➤ Chapter Three: **A Competitive Economy**

- **Problem:** The prevailing communist mentality stifles new businesses.

- **Solution:** The government must relinquish some control in favor of a more competitive economy. Entrepreneurs must then seize that opportunity.

➤ Chapter Four: **Expedite Systems**

- **Problem:** A frustrating amount of bureaucracy causes many aspiring entrepreneurs to give up early in the process.

- **Solution:** Secure automation tools, such as online business license applications, should be implemented to expedite time-consuming systems.

➤ Chapter Five: **The Tax Burden**

- **Problem:** The taxation system is rife with corruption and inefficiency, breeding distrust between the government and its citizens.

- **Solution:** Large-scale tax reforms must introduce better tax exemptions and tax return policies so that business owners feel proud, rather than ashamed, of taking advantage.

➤ Chapter Six: **Accessible Financing**

- **Problem:** With limited investment options and credit systems, the reliance on bank-provided funding means that startups have a difficult time launching, let alone scaling.

- **Solution:** Laws must be revised to invite foreign investors and banks, introduce a more effective credit system, and diversify ways to receive financing.

> Chapter Seven: **Invest in Learning**

- **Problem:** Graduates often leave college without proper professional skills, meaning companies must train new hires from scratch, not in *policy* but in *methodology*.

- **Solution:** As Ethiopia continues to improve its education system, companies are responsible for providing opportunities, investing in staff development, and guiding the workforce to a place of increased knowledge and expertise.

> Chapter Eight: **High-Performing Teams**

- **Problem:** Ethiopian business culture tends to be *laissez faire*, with a lack of skilled employees, high absenteeism rates, and low motivation.

- **Solution:** Companies need leaders who empower employees by instilling goals and milestones, structure, and most importantly, purpose-driven work.

> Chapter Nine: **Export African Talent**

- **Problem:** Although outsourcing opportunities would radically change the economy, challenges such as digital illiteracy and internet reliability discourage foreign businesses from expanding into Ethiopia.

> **Solution:** Ethiopia is a "sleeping giant" in outsourcing. Opening the economy would revolutionize daily life, be a strategic advantage for foreign companies, and make a lasting impact on Africa as a whole.

While Ethiopia may not have the same professional ecosystem in 15, 10, or even 5 years from now, the experiences outlined here are timeless, revealing universal truths all entrepreneurs, African or otherwise, experience sometime in their lives regarding perseverance, relationships, responsibility, sacrifice, and quick action. Many carry the negative perception that change can never occur in Ethiopia, that the challenges are simply insurmountable. To that, I say: With more professionals and entrepreneurs, whether aspiring or seasoned, raising their voices and making a commitment to addressing these obstacles head-on, any issue can be rectified. Now, with a youth population of 41 million Ethiopian citizens aged 10 years and above, the country can take advantage of this workforce, maximize this potential, and foster wide-scale national change.

My hope is that this book inspires the next wave of entrepreneurs to take on the risk and understand that their country and its people are worth the effort. With more ideas, more creativity, and more action, Ethiopia's private sector and economy can flourish. Rather than ceaseless resiliency, it is now time for sustainable prosperity.

After all, is that not the definition of an entrepreneur—one who identifies and solves major problems to influence great change in their communities, their countries, and the world?

CHAPTER ONE

Accidental Entrepreneur

Haile Gebrselassie is considered one of the greatest runners in world history with numerous victories and world records in almost every long-distance and middle-distance event.[1] I have the highest respect for his company, Haile Hotel & Resorts, which can be found across major tourist destinations, namely Arba Minch, Adama, Hawassa, Gondar, and Ziway (Batu). In addition to also owning Yaya Africa Athletics Village, Haile invests in various sectors, including commercial real estate, coffee, and automotive trading and assembly. His efforts have created thousands of jobs and generated millions of birr in tax revenue for his country.[2] Olympian, world champion, and entrepreneur are all titles earned through his simple philosophy: "Win for yourself."[3]

In the small farming village of Asela, 150 miles south of Addis Ababa, a seven-year-old Haile Gebrselassie crouched down in a field, far away from his family's house. He turned up the volume on the family radio he'd stolen away, listening to Miruts Yifter's 10,000-meter final in Moscow. Yifter was an accomplished Ethiopian long-distance runner and, importantly, Haile's hero. Growing up on rural farmland, Haile performed the strenuous but essential work of plowing fields behind an ox, fetching water miles away, and tending to cattle at an early age. Six days a week at 6:30 a.m., Haile ran 10 kilometers to school each day and another 10 kilometers back home. For Yifter to be celebrated for what he did everyday out of necessity—running—he thought, "How is it possible? How can one man be so special?"

Then Haile had the next logical thought: "I want to be like Miruts Yifter." At seven years old, he defined his life path.

Haile had risked a great deal to listen to the race, seeing as his father maintained strict control over the radio and its battery life. In the late 1970s and early 1980s, Ethiopia struggled to stabilize in the face of the emperor's removal. Counterrevolutionary groups would form and then break apart, and the redistribution of land posed a great threat, especially with Haile's family being farmers. With the rise of a socialist economy, Haile's father held the radio close, only using it for news and never entertainment. Every evening after the news, he took the batteries out of the back and hid them, ensuring they lasted for as long as possible. To earn money to replace them was a difficult task.

Knowing his father despised thieves and would be upset if he found out, Haile still stole the radio and its batteries, feeling, even then, that listening was somehow cosmically important. He was right. In the last 300 meters of the race, "Yifter the Shifter" changed gears and darted ahead of his four opponents, becoming the 10,000-meter champion.

"An Ethiopian," Haile thought. "An Ethiopian *like me*."

The rest is history, with Haile spending two decades as one of the most decorated runners in the world. He competed in four Olympics, won two Olympic gold medals in 1996 and 2000, and was a five-time World Champion in 1993, 1995, 1997, and 1999.[4] He broke 61 Ethiopian national records, set 27 world records, and was declared one of the 100 most influential Africans by *New African Magazine*.[5] Retiring from professional running in 2015, Haile set his sights on other pursuits, notably the successful hotel chain he founded in 2010.

Spending much of his career staying in overseas hotels, Haile noticed that many of the services he used were unavailable in Ethiopia. His retirement offered him the opportunity to fill that market gap, and now, he has procured hotels and resorts, a real estate business, a coffee plantation, and a share in a Hyundai car-assembly plant—all of which employ more than 3,000 Ethiopians. He even opened the first privately owned movie theater, Alem Cinema Hall, in a country that, before then, did not have a film industry.[6] Haile's story is one of strife, humble means, hard work, and what I call "accidental entrepreneurship," the act of waking up one day and realizing that the way you *thought* you'd make a difference could really be multiplied and maximized if you owned a business.

"We need Ethiopian businessmen who aren't afraid to change traditions," Haile has said. "But they can't simply follow American or British ways. They have to remain Ethiopian; they have to live and act as Ethiopians do."[7]

An inspiring quote, one that harkens back to the powerful image of Haile running 10 kilometers to school every day, his left arm bent in a distinct posture in order to hold his textbooks. As an adult, this posture would become his calling card, the very trait that characterized and defined him as a runner—who became a champion not *despite* but *because of* his Ethiopian heritage.

My Dream

I am an accidental entrepreneur. When I first established my company, IE Networks, I did not do so with a grandiose vision, idea, or desire for elevated status. Rather, IE Networks was born as a way to manage my part-time freelance work. If you had asked me whether I imagined my current career 15 or 20 years ago, I would tell you that I never did. That is not to chastise or diminish the excellent work done by entrepreneurs who have great ambitions and want to change the world. To them, I say well done and keep it up; you are needed more than you know. However, not everyone must enter a career in business as a natural-born, bold, and inspired visionary. In most cases, it is enough to strive for market disruption, for the pursuit of knowledge, or to become a better person than you were yesterday. I would hope that by doing so, more people would find themselves at the helm of a self-owned business.

I have always said that who you should compete with is not another person, but your prior self. Following this principle is how I found myself as the only CCIE-certified individual in Ethiopia at 24 years old, with numerous opportunities in arm's reach. I first worked at a private IT company, moved to a federal role while working for a government data center operations, and then, in 2008, accepted a position as a telecom consultant, building nationwide internet and telephone systems as part of the Next Generation Network. Each job supplied a consistent, reliable salary, so when I decided to start a business in addition to my full-time career, very little risk was involved.

My CCIE status earned me a reputation. Back then, such standing, knowledge, and experience were rare, particularly in Africa, and even now, CCIE-certified experts remain an elite group. Whenever a government office, university, bank, or other organization sought to establish a network, I would be called to help with the design, testing, supervision, and/or quality control as an independent contractor. Not only was I working every minute of my full-time job during the week, but I also worked long hours in the evenings and on the weekends as well, earning additional income here and there. My Saturdays and Sundays belonged to the Ministry of Revenue, universities, and the Main Department for Immigration and Nationality Affairs.

As far back as I can remember, I have always wanted to excel at whatever I did. If tasks needed doing, I wanted to do them—and do them in a better, more efficient way than anyone had thought of before. I believe everything necessitates above-average effort for above-average output. If an objective required more than eight hours of work, I would rearrange my schedule just so I could complete it excellently, not adequately. If it took 10 hours, 12 hours, or even 16 hours, then I would not stop until I saw it accomplished. Even lunch breaks seemed to define my work ethic. Whenever coworkers would drink coffee or eat together, I would join them and their conversations, but then, I would return to work in the allotted time while others would extend 10-minute breaks to 30 minutes, an hour, or even a few hours. It was fine for them to enjoy the camaraderie, but I was driven by the need to resolve whatever task or problem I was engaged in.

Do not misunderstand. My dedication was not motivated by a paycheck or how much overtime I could accrue. My experience, notably in government roles, showed me that I had something to contribute and that I could facilitate a wide-scale impact on Ethiopian business culture. From these eye-opening experiences, I saw, for the first time, that if we ran our country like a business, Ethiopia could find innovative solutions to its core problems and center itself around a common mission— just as a business does.

My additional freelance work enabled me to do more in pursuit of this future (although I did not acknowledge that at the time) and to execute fulfilling work. I remember one incident in which the passport system for the national immigration office went down. Knowing my name and credentials, the office called me and explained the situation, but unfortunately, I was 600 kilometers (about 373 miles) away from the city and not able to respond as quickly as necessary. The office representatives assured me that the distance would not be a problem, paid for my airplane ticket, and even sent a VIP car to pick me up from the airport. Both the urgency and reliance on *my* services showed me that my expertise was appreciated and needed, even on a national level. I took this as a sign to continue accepting freelance projects and responsibilities, watching how the problems I fixed created a ripple effect for how many federal operations functioned.

As I took on more and more work, I recognized the need to establish a separate business entity. A 35% tax was deducted for each project, but if I had an official company, only 2% of that income would be withheld for taxes and I could declare my expenses. The only problem was I did not have nearly enough time to go to the government offices and obtain a business license, in addition to the other paperwork I needed. As I remained busy every day, evening, and weekend, my wife saw how hard I was pushing myself, and she volunteered to apply in my place. My wife started the seemingly endless and complicated process of getting a business license in Ethiopia. These days, the business license application process may only take one or two weeks, but back then, we waited for months.

Even after waiting and completing endless paperwork to finalize the company's name and business license, I still did not consider myself an entrepreneur. I was a skilled engineer who wanted to distinguish myself by one day moving to the US, living in Silicon Valley, and joining a large corporation such as Google or Cisco. That was my dream—not to set up a company in Ethiopia. However, because the government had sponsored me for the exam, I signed an agreement that stated I would serve at least three years in the country as repayment for travel costs and the exam fee. If I did not serve the three years, the contract positioned my mother as the guarantor, stating that she would have to repay the government's expenses. But even beyond the collateral clause, my interest was not to leave my country and work elsewhere just yet. I wanted to serve the government that gave me a life-changing opportunity, and I wished to honor my commitment. Therefore, my plan, at least initially, was to work in Ethiopia for three years and then move to another country, seeing as I could find a job anywhere in the world.

Little did I know that my dream would soon change as the first two employees I hired turned into 10, then 20, and so on. Years later, IE Networks now employs 200 individuals and has generated millions of USD in annual revenue—all while centering itself around one central purpose that has redefined how I view Ethiopia, my home and where I will continue to live well into the future.

Scaling IE Network

It has been more than 16 years since the establishment of IE Networks. A B2B company, we engage directly with businesses, serving companies, banks, governmental organizations, and international corporations. With a focus on maximizing value as a service-oriented solutions provider, our offerings range from enterprise network services and business automation intelligence to smart infrastructure and cloud services. As the primary enterprise solutions provider in Ethiopia, IE Networks aims to influence African industry through hard work, competence, consistency, integrity, and a disciplined work culture. Our efforts affect the work ethics of our society and the overall technological development of Ethiopia in the long term.

Reaching this level of impact, i.e., scaling the company to its current size and influence, came slowly and naturally. A startup only begins to flourish after establishing offerings, a proof of concept, and a foundational consumer base. The chaos demands very little hierarchy, if one exists at all, as employees must work together in a myriad of different departments and capacities. In order to scale, you must adopt a different mindset, instead shifting to a more organized structure with defined job responsibilities. Like most business owners who start as experts in their fields, I struggled to delegate tasks when first forming this structure. Everyone came to me for help, and I made all of the decisions, falling into the age-old trap of working *in* the business rather than *on* it. Managing 10 or even 20 people was not too difficult, but when IE Networks started to approach 100 employees, I realized that I had to trust others to take responsibility. For others to do that, we needed a proper hierarchy, a refined process, and thorough documentation. We also needed departments, such as sales, engineering, and accounting; procedures, such as email check-ins and weekly meetings; and a much bigger office space.

One advantage of the developed world is easy access to skilled managers. In Ethiopia, however, almost no hiring candidates hold MBAs or prior management experience. Filling a management position with an adept, experienced professional typically means hiring an individual at entry level and then mentoring and training them to fill a managerial role years later. Simply posting a job listing with certain requirements will not net someone with 10 years of prior experience, master's degrees or certifications, or history with specific technologies. Due to many societal reasons (but primarily educational flaws, covered more thoroughly in chapter seven), Ethiopian workers, in my experience, are more of an investment, where nurturing growth is the responsibility of the employer.

Despite the limited hiring pool, I have been fortunate to find and cultivate relationships with many dedicated team members. Together, we have created a business culture outside the norm yet one that instills us with energy and purpose. Compared to other companies, IE Networks has earned a reputation for being detail-oriented, structured, and meticulous, but that is because we take our roles very seriously. IE Networks is often an employee's first exposure to a high-functioning, high-achieving organization with expectations, deadlines, and a mission to which they can contribute. Instead of the prominent, laborious jobs, such as agriculture or construction, or motiveless jobs, such as tedious administrative work, my hope is that IE Networks encourages employees to strive for more, beyond the first categories on Maslow's hierarchy of needs (psychological and safety needs) and toward belongingness, purpose, and self-actualization.

IE Networks's mission to empower team members, deliver quality and client-centered services, and redefine Ethiopia's business culture as a whole, both to support future entrepreneurs and provide opportunities for the evolving workforce, is what gets me out of bed in the morning. I am immensely proud of the impact we have made and continue to make every day. Especially after voicing the company's story on podcasts and interviews, several young people have greeted me at airports, restaurants, and other public spaces to tell me they are inspired. On days when I become overwhelmed with the countless challenges Ethiopians must overcome in order to carve out a functional, well-operating society, I see these young people, many of whom are aspiring entrepreneurs, and I am reminded of how achievement is not only possible but probable for us.

Quitter or Achiever?

Most Ethiopians do not start businesses. In fact, most Ethiopians do not see self-employment as a viable option at all. What few entrepreneurs exist typically open or inherit small, local shops, helping their parents or relatives sell agricultural products they grew themselves. Others may perform certain types of work within the community, such as tailoring or laundry services. Commonly, educated Ethiopians are not the ones who pursue entrepreneurial ventures; those with degrees tend to either find high-paying jobs within the country or leave to find work in other nations. Many do not explore the viability of accepting risk and starting a business, and if they do try self-employment, they often cannot support themselves on the little pay they receive before establishing their brand and consumer pool.

The problem when living in a poor country is that money seems like a solution for every issue. This misconception originates from the diaspora of US tourists and missionaries. Many Americans will realize how far the US dollar extends in Ethiopia and begin spending a tremendous amount of money with their credit cards, giving gifts, and attending expensive parties and attractions. For anyone who has never been outside of Ethiopia, the extravagant display of wealth appears to be a solution. "If I go to the US," they think, "all of my problems will be solved."

Attaining funds in the US is no simple feat, however. Most Ethiopian immigrants, when moving to the US, hold proportionally low-income jobs (with respect to the American income perspective and difference) that demand strenuous hours and extensive labor. When traveling to major US cities, I try to observe Ethiopian people and go to Ethiopian restaurants when and where I can. Of the Ethiopians I speak to and hear of, a low percentage secure jobs in large corporations. The majority tend to work as taxi drivers, valets, housekeepers, and servers—admirable work but hardly the opportunities they hoped to find after leaving Ethiopia.

When Americans come to Ethiopia, why do they not tell the truth about life in the US? Is this part of the reason Ethiopians set their sights on overseas nations, rather than their home country? According to the Missing Migrants Project, more than 900 Ethiopians have died on migration routes in the past decade, with Africa being the second-deadliest region for immigrants and seeing more than 9,000 migration-related deaths documented since 2014.[8] Too many Ethiopians die each year from life-threatening attempts at US or European immigration, all because they believe in an earthly heaven in the West. Yet, opportunity exists at home given that we begin supplying the necessary resources and support. There is no better way to achieve your ambitions than to build something sustainable for yourself, your family, and your community.

Only very recently has the idea of entrepreneurship and self-sustainability entered public attention. Really, the concept of *staying and building a life in Ethiopia* has only recently entered the conversation as well. I will never forget the first time I traveled to the US for a short, two-week stay. When I returned to Ethiopia according to schedule, my friends and relatives asked me, "What are you? Crazy? Why did you fly back?" They questioned my decision and urged me to rethink, the expectation being that I would stay overseas and send money back home. I had much, much higher objectives at the time, and in hindsight, I am glad I pursued those long-term goals. Life in the US would not have been as rewarding as my time in Ethiopia.

With entrepreneurship, every challenge brings opportunity. And every day, it seems, brings new challenges. Even so, my life is one of freedom—freedom to own my own business, drive my own mission, create my own rules and standards, and uplift those around me. I have the honor of making a change and seeing the effects of that change. My impact extends beyond a nine-to-five job; I pave the way for others after me and galvanize innovation on a national and global level. Born in a poor family, I have also overcome poverty and transformed my life as well as the lives of my family members. Very few people have the chance to do that, especially in a developing country. Every day is exciting and rewarding.

My work at IE Networks and beyond is about fulfilling my purpose. Once I met basic income needs, I could have stopped growing the company and lived a well-rounded life. But once I reached the quality of life I sought, my goals transformed beyond financial security. When you help others, create an environment where young people will benefit, and see the growth of new hires into accomplished and capable professionals, you realize how you have changed someone else's life. And it becomes addictive.

Every year, I try to visit a new country to experience new cultures and environments, and every year, I am greeted with the same surprise when I return to Ethiopia. The more I travel, the more I ask myself: Why would I migrate to a place where I would have to become a different person and adapt to a foreign culture? The payoff is insignificant compared to my life and legacy in Ethiopia, where I am positioned to make a difference for entrepreneurs and engineers as I grow IE Networks.

I have learned that a business grows almost identically to a child. You proudly watch it take its first steps and guide it through kindergarten and its early years, but you also look forward to the day it matures and grows beyond any expectations you could have conceived. The work is too interesting and thrilling to abandon, with the early challenges of a business greatly differing from the challenges of 10 employees and then changing again when you reach 100. There is always a new problem to solve and a new system to develop. Entrepreneurs certainly never get bored.

Many obstacles still limit the immense potential of IE Networks, but despite these, which I cover in detail in the following chapters, I continue toward a sole objective: to be the living proof of a successful Ethiopian entrepreneur. While many challenges exist, there are even more ways to solve them, and the people who strive for change will gain the voice to inform policies and address challenges. My voice alone is not enough. More business leaders and entrepreneurs must join the cause and face these challenges on the ground; only then will we resolve the barriers and hindrances in our country.

For now, all any of us can do is wake up every morning and ask ourselves:

"Am I a quitter? Or am I an achiever?"

CHAPTER TWO

Beyond Just Enough

A revolution unlike anything Ethiopia has ever seen lies on the horizon. To understand it, we must first understand its past—a long history that begins alongside civilization.

The sub-Saharan kingdom of Aksum emerged as a well-established Ethiopian trading state during the first century C.E. Located in the highlands of Tigray, the empire thrived for centuries with a peak population of 20,000 and vast trade routes linking the Roman Empire to the Middle East and India. With trading partners like Egypt, South Arabia, India, China, and the Byzantine Romans, trades primarily included gold and ivory but also exports such as tortoise shells, rhinoceros horns, frankincense, myrrh, emeralds, salt, and live animals. With regard to its elaborate monuments and historic written language, perhaps the most relevant accomplishment was its currency. Aksum was the first African territory to mint its own coins—an astounding fact.[1] Ethiopia was one of the first to pioneer capitalist currency, yet it struggles today to streamline payments for goods and services and overcome limiting ideals surrounding money.

As compelling as this knowledge is, I tell the story of Aksum not as an entertaining history lesson but more as a commentary on *tradition*, a theme that will reoccur in this book time and again. Young Western countries, such as the US and Canada, which are only about 250 and 150 years old respectively, cannot fathom a national history expanding thousands of years. What might these countries look like with over 3,000 years of known history? How might they operate? What culture might form, born out of centuries of conflict and prosperity alike?

I say this only to present a dichotomy of tradition: one between *remembering* and *forgetting*. How can we *remember* the publicly owned past but *forget* that our roots lie in business?

Perhaps this is because Ethiopia's struggle against communist dictatorship occurred in much more recent history. It began in the build-up to World War II when Benito Mussolini set his sights on Ethiopia, known as Abyssinia at the time. Italian fascist troops marched over the border in October 1935.[2] Although Ethiopia has never officially been colonized, this military campaign took control of much of the country for nearly five years while the Ethiopian army struggled to combat the invaders. As the Second World War progressed and Italian forces expanded their presence in North Africa, the British led offensive maneuvers, and bit by bit, their combined efforts pushed the Italian troops back. The 1941 Battle of Keren was a pivotal moment as British and Ethiopian regiments ran the Italians out of Eritrea, just north of Ethiopia. Following these continued losses, the Italian governor stationed in North Africa entered negotiations for surrender.

Ethiopia's involvement in the war elevated its presence on a global scale and solidified its independent statehood, particularly following the Anglo-Ethiopian agreement signed on January 31, 1942.[3] Despite the losses suffered during the war, Ethiopia experienced many developments, such as the revised Ethiopian constitution and the first conference of the Organization of African Unity in 1963.[4] While each effort attempted to empower and represent African voices in the global discussion, peace was not long enjoyed as a widespread famine took hold from 1973 to 1974.[5]

Founded on Marxist theories, a group called "the Derg" appealed to struggling Ethiopians by promising them structure, support, and a voice in the government. Colonel Mengistu Haile Mariam established himself as the leader, though he was unable to maintain full control, particularly as drought and famine continued into the 1980s. With these intense shortcomings and dwindling satisfaction, unrest grew. The Ethiopian People's Revolutionary Party (EPRP) rebelled against the Derg, resulting in a long period of violence.

Following the end of this regime, the Ethiopian People's Revolutionary Democratic Front (EPRDF) introduced a period of transition, stepping forward to democratize Ethiopia with a new constitution in 1994 and numerous reforms such as elections and economic policies.[6] Decades later, when Abiy Ahmed, PhD, was elected as leader of EPRDF and prime minister in 2018, many Ethiopians embraced his united and prosperous movement that attempted to bring the country back to peace in the face of enduring inter-ethnic clashes and political instability. His inaugural address promised a period of advancement and innovation:

> We will leverage our diversity which at times manifests in the form of difference of opinion. And in nations, differences are assets, not liabilities. We are a budding democracy, and it is in our differences that we often come up with the most groundbreaking solutions to existing problems. Ethiopia is our home and the only one we have. We need to find more issues that unite us than divide us. We Ethiopians

need democracy, freedom, and liberty, and we are entitled to it![7]

In light of a conflicted history, Ethiopia is now moving toward an open market with a focus on encouraging foreign investors, improving the ease of doing business, and accelerating accession to the World Trade Organization. Prime Minister Abiy is not making wide-sweeping promises from the pulpit— he has taken concrete steps, such as the development of the Ethiopian Securities Exchange (ESX) and awarding a degree of privatization to some state-owned industries (airlines and telecommunications) to encourage foreign investment and support domestic private sectors.

Ethiopia is considered an emerging power because of its ongoing development, with an average annual economic growth rate of nearly 10% over the past 15 years.[8] Much of this is a result of public infrastructure investments, particularly from FDI in agriculture and manufacturing, which has provided jobs and improved the quality of life across the nation. As the population shifts younger, Ethiopia is on the cusp of becoming one of the largest labor markets in the world. With 128.6 million people and a median age of 18.8, the country brims with potential.[9] There is growth at every turn, from policy reforms to educational legislation to foreign direct investment. As the poverty line steadily decreases and progress begins to occur in crucial industries, the backbone of the country strengthens as a whole.

From such a 30,000-foot view, Ethiopia's history is dense and complex, not only spanning back to the beginning of civilization but also delving into the nuanced and difficult topics of communism and capitalism, human rights, and government control. One book cannot hope to dissect every detail, and thankfully, this book does not attempt to. Rather, I hope to place stability, in all its forms, at the center of progress. And the key to stability is financial strength, proper access to essential needs such as healthcare and education, and a feeling of political security from civilians.

In essence, there are many problems—but only one true solution.

Problem

Moving forward requires recognizing Ethiopia's limitations, both from a federal and individual level. From a government standpoint, legislation must enable changemakers to identify issues and integrate sustainable solutions. These changemakers must then be willing to find a purpose or cause, let it drive their actions, and overcome steep barriers by moving fearlessly through, in many cases, unchartered waters.

In other words, an increase in entrepreneurial opportunities within the country of Ethiopia has the potential to solve inefficiencies in every sector of the economy. But first, in order to *solve* the problems, we must *understand* the problems— and importantly, from where the problems stem.

➤ **Education**

The United Nations Children's Fund (UNICEF) states that 90% of 10-year-olds in Ethiopia do not know how to read a simple, text-based sentence. Although most children enroll in school, only about 33% proceed to secondary school, a critical factor being that living in rural settings makes it more difficult for children to continue. Because of this, at least 13 million children are out of school, and an estimated 3.5 million additional children are at risk of dropping out. Nearly half of both groups are girls.[10]

For many decades, educational options beyond K–12 were also limited. During the rule of the last emperor, two universities existed in the country. Anyone who sought more education had to take their ambitions and ideas abroad. In the communist Derg period, many soldiers who became government leaders only had a high-school-level education, and higher education became extremely discouraged. The two existing universities fell into decline.

Gradual improvement followed the end of the military regime, but the true surge in education occurred after Meles Zenawi's government revitalized the education system, developing a total of 42 universities and specifically encouraging engineering and business students in order to change the economic landscape.[11] I was part of this education movement, having received a strong secondary education that positioned me to attend Mekelle University for a degree in electrical engineering.

There is still much work to be done in the way of education. The momentum of reform experienced a slight setback due to continued armed conflicts, drought and famine, and the COVID-19 pandemic.[12] Plus, hundreds of college graduates are flooding the labor market, and without enough job openings available, many either leave the country for other opportunities or work in labor-intensive jobs, leaving their knowledge hanging on the wall beside their diplomas. The value of education is perceived as low by the general population since the follow-through of a job is still so limited, making the argument for education more difficult to justify.

Yet, these challenges have not extinguished the potential of the next generation. Enrollment is on the rise and stands to move Ethiopia in the right direction. Organizations such as UNICEF have had an immense impact, especially in rural areas. UNICEF has held a presence in Ethiopia for over 70 years, helping the gradual transformation of education by ensuring support for students, schools, and teachers with materials, training, and technical support.[13] As much as I admire the work being done here, I also wonder what privately owned, local Ethiopian companies could do to transform the space. How could more teachers and more impassioned individuals from a variety of backgrounds join ideas to make learning more accessible across Ethiopia? What businesses or nonprofit organizations could be established to address key challenges and ensure children have textbooks, laptops, transportation, school supplies, and other needed resources? What *other* companies would be needed, in addition to these organizations, to make this a reality?

The leaders of tomorrow are shaped through learning. How could private businesses exponentially promote and fortify that learning, beyond what public companies already provide?

Healthcare

Compared to other countries, Ethiopia's rural population faces limited access to safe water, housing, sanitation, food, and healthcare. Despite modern investments by the government to improve conditions, the country still grapples with key health concerns, including high rates of HIV/AIDS, infant mortality, TB, malaria, hepatitis B and C, and respiratory infections. Non-infectious diseases, such as cancer, diabetes, heart diseases, and high blood pressure, also show above-average numbers.

The rise of health risks can be attributed to many factors. First, the Derg era, when many doctors emigrated and left a substantial shortage from which the country is still attempting to recover. As a response, many medical schools produce general practitioners instead of specialists. There is a rising demand year after year, and the shortage of doctors, equipment, and drugs continues to create new problems.

Second, Ethiopia's healthcare system is not accessible to all citizens. While the system includes hospitals, primary health centers, and clinics, the only hospitals that have physicians onsite at all times are in major cities, primarily Addis Ababa. This leaves rural areas extremely vulnerable with limited access to care and medication, and with most healthcare facilities in Ethiopia being owned by the government, progress is slow.

As of early 2024, the following *public* healthcare facilities existed:

- **Health Posts**: 17,534 available and 77 under construction
- **Health Centers**: 3,587 available and 89 under construction
- **Hospitals**: 3,643 available and 57 under construction

In comparison, the following *private* facilities were in operation:

- **Private Clinics**: 3,867 available
- **Private Hospitals**: 43 available[14]

Several obvious solutions to the healthcare dilemma exist: more private hospitals, accessibility, physicians, specialists, nurses, process improvement, and financial support from all sides. Multiple global organizations have been facilitating such work in Ethiopia for generations, and paired with the domestic work of the Ministry of Health and the Ethiopia Food and Drug Authority, the country has seen major improvements in the past decade, increasing the availability of much-needed medical drugs, supplies, and devices.

Though most transformation must come from within the health sector, I would also like to point outward, toward the work done by companies outside the industry. One company in particular is soleRebels, the world's fastest-growing African footwear brand.

After growing up in an impoverished area of Addis Ababa, the owner of soleRebels, Bethlehem Tilahun Alemu, opened a small footwear workshop on her grandmother's land in 2005, using zero carbon emissions and local materials to produce her shoes. Now, soleRebels is the first African consumer brand to ever open standalone branded retail stores internationally, with stores open in the US, Germany, Greece, Singapore, Spain, Switzerland, and Taiwan.[15]

Perhaps the most admirable trait of soleRebels, besides its inspiring rise to success, is its dedication to providing healthcare, education, and financial stability within Ethiopia.[16] Positioning employees as its most valuable assets, soleRebels offers:

- above-average salaries that are four to five times the legal minimum wage and over three times the average salary,
- medical insurance that covers 100% of employee's and their family's healthcare expenses, and
- even transportation to and from work for employees with disabilities.

It's amazing that one company, outside the healthcare sector, can influence such monumental change for the health of its employees.

➤ Infrastructure

In 2023, the Ethiopian construction industry generated $69.5 billion USD.[17] Through ambitious housing projects, large-scale commercial construction, and energy and utilities construction such as the Grand Ethiopian Renaissance Dam, the economic and physical landscape of Ethiopia is experiencing tremendous change, especially in the capital city of Addis Ababa. This is in no small part due to the work and influence of Chinese construction companies.

Since the turn of the century, Chinese companies and investors have maintained a significant presence in Ethiopia with support from their government, which, in 2014, announced a long-term plan to upgrade Ethiopia's infrastructure and continue the China-Africa partnership.[18] Much of the construction in Ethiopia is led by foreign contractors with Chinese contractors at the helm, though their workforce is predominantly local. Frustrated by the work of native Ethiopian contractors, builders now turn to foreign companies for parks, railways, airports, roads, dams, and other public infrastructure projects. More than 1,300 projects were in the process of being constructed by Chinese contractors in 2023, a number that rose from 415 in 2011.

Construction officials put forth several reasons for choosing foreign contractors over domestic ones, including that local contractors tend to:
- delay projects,
- increase costs,
- deliver low-quality work, and
- lack the appropriate technology, coordination, and skill.[19]

While I certainly welcome and encourage the entry of foreign companies into Ethiopia, I am also a firm believer in economic competition. Without overly simplifying this complicated problem, the issue of Chinese involvement in construction boils down to process improvement. How can Ethiopians begin to compete? What needs to change concerning work ethic and standard procedures? More importantly, how do Ethiopian contractors find a way to differentiate themselves and give the government a reason to solicit their services over their Chinese counterparts?

More entrepreneurial opportunities would transform the construction sector. With access to foreign currency and better loan opportunities from banks—in addition to more businesses striving to make a difference, standing out from the status quo, and reshaping the industry's culture—Ethiopia would witness healthy competition in its economy. Competition that would spur each company to better its services, reduce its prices, and find new, innovative ways of staying ahead.

Agriculture

Ethiopia's agriculture sector accounts for about 40% of annual gross domestic product (GDP).[20] The coffee industry put Ethiopia on the map, beginning back in the 1450s and since becoming a longstanding pillar of the heavily agriculture-dependent economy.[21] Even during the COVID pandemic in 2020 and 2021, nearly 15 million Ethiopian farmers were responsible for 280,607 metric tons of coffee leaving the country for faraway ports.[22] More recently, according to a statement by the Ethiopian Coffee and Tea Authority, Ethiopia exported 298,500 metric tons of coffee during the 2023/24 fiscal year. This resulted in $218 million in income, a record amount.[23]

The agricultural industry is an undeniable economic staple. Even so, it is not prioritized as an essential asset and supported by improved technology or a determined drive to optimize processes. Instead, the farming sector is dominated by inefficient hand tools. Not only does a reliance on manual labor increase work hazards and put physical strain on farmers, but these hand tools also perpetuate poor quality of work, maintain poverty, and repel youth from wanting jobs in agriculture. Efforts are being made to mechanize the industry and therefore "improve the overall efficiency of food systems, reduce the costs of producing outputs and providing services, enhance economies of scale, and raise labor productivity and incomes." More mechanized agriculture, such as modern barns, tractors, spraying machines, water pumps, and combiners, are being imported, but it will require farmer implementation for these new technologies to take hold.[24]

It is clear that agriculture is a large opportunity to innovate and imbue new ideas, harness revenue, and create more opportunities. Entrepreneurship in this sector would help to revolutionize the country as a whole since much of the world relies on Ethiopia's agricultural outputs. With innovation, there is an opportunity for the young Ethiopian population to transform a labor-intensive, back-breaking industry into a lucrative, streamlined business that benefits the highly respectable and essential work of farmers—an industry that keeps food on the table, yes, but also sustains the lifeblood of the nation.

Solution

Ethiopia is not only one of the oldest countries in the world but also the oldest independent country in Africa, having never been colonized by European forces.[25] While the effects of this have preserved treasured cultural and historical customs and practices integral to Ethiopia's heritage, legacy, and identity—a tradition-oriented mindset comes with an enduring resistance to change. As a result, much of the Ethiopian workforce does not question the nation's poverty status, instead falling into a sort of complacency and taking comfort in the status quo. Tradition tells families to be thankful for food on the table and clothes on their backs, no matter if they only eat once a day or have one new outfit per year. With an overreliance on agriculture, Ethiopians rarely fret or worry about where their next meal will come from due to the country's moderate climate, free of cold or hot seasons. If a person has soil, they can plant and grow *just enough* food to sustain themselves.

As an entrepreneur, I see opportunities for great innovation that would radically change daily life where many see *just enough* resources to scrape by. The need for private businesses to invent new solutions and find better ways of living is no longer a distant hope. It is needed, and it is urgent. Yet, despite the enormous potential for successful entrepreneurial pursuits, the majority of Ethiopians hold a distinctly unique but very detrimental mindset: one that says being poor in this life will lead to riches in the afterlife.

As one of the earliest Christian countries (with Christianity becoming the official state religion in the fourth century), religion heavily influences the mentality of many, particularly a verse from Matthew 19:24: "It is easier for a camel to go through the eye of a needle, than for a rich man to enter into the kingdom of God."[26]

Many do not want to build a business or even become middle-class because they expect to enjoy luxuries in the afterlife. The effect of such a mentality is clear: Ethiopia is one of the poorest countries in the world, a status we should no longer be comfortable with. Despite this, I often find people around me become uncomfortable when I say that Ethiopians work hard and should be rewarded for their efforts. I do not encourage a selfish pursuit of riches and vanity; I simply want to introduce purpose and passion into others' lives. I want to show Ethiopians that it is possible to hold true to their faith and still embrace opportunity. My opinion may be uncommon, but I do believe people can work hard and still do good with their money.

From the economy to core mindsets, Ethiopia is deeply immersed in a period of transition. While recent history has been tumultuous, the past 20 years have been a time of growth and development, laying the foundation for the future. The transition to a stable economy may take 10 to 20 years before we see the payoff, but reform, education, and foreign investment are the start. The work is both possible and necessary—for every entrepreneur that plants business roots in Ethiopia, hundreds of families could experience change. If this pattern is repeated across all industries, Ethiopia will shift from a country known for its poverty to one of prosperity. That has been a driving force behind my work and continues to push my business ventures forward.

When people hear that I own a business, they assume I grew up privileged or that I am somehow politically aligned— otherwise, there is no explanation in their mind for how an independent Ethiopian could create a successful business. This is a self-imposed, limiting mindset that needs to be dismantled to allow more Ethiopians to pursue the opportunities waiting out there. The industries are changing and growth is happening; we should not watch from the sidelines.

I want to evolve the idea of what it means to be Ethiopian—and the only way possible is through new innovations, creative ideas, and collaboration. In other words, entrepreneurship.

CHAPTER THREE
A Competitive Economy

Prior to 2019, Ethiopia had one of the fastest-growing economies in the world, partially due to its investments in public, rather than private, infrastructure. The appointment of Abiy Ahmed as prime minister in 2018 only seemed to demonstrate that the country was moving in the right direction as Abiy intended to further build out the economy. He planned to improve the investment climate and turn state-owned enterprises into private businesses, some of which involved the telecom, airline, shipping and logistics, power, and sugar industries. However, any growth strategies abruptly paused with the onset of COVID-19 in 2019, in addition to prolonged civil unrest. Now, with the conclusion of the war and COVID-19 posing less of a threat, Prime Minister Abiy hopes to continue supporting the economy and privatization efforts because, as he and I both recognize—a limited private sector stifles entrepreneurship and, therefore, inhibits the success of a nation.

In 2022, Ethiopia had a real GDP of 6%, greater than the 4% average for East Africa.[1] However, the economy has historically been fueled by the agriculture industry, contributing nearly 40% to GDP, employing 80% of the total population, and generating 90% of Ethiopia's foreign currency from exports.[2] With Ethiopia being Africa's largest coffee producer and the world's fifth largest exporter of Arabica coffee, the coffee industry generates approximately 30–35% of Ethiopia's total export earnings and contributes to the livelihoods of a quarter of the population.[3] Smallholder farming accounts for approximately 95% of agricultural production and 85% of total employment, making agriculture the most valuable and long-standing industry.[4]

Although agriculture has been a fundamental pillar of Ethiopia's economy for centuries, the services industry is now growing as well due to the expansion of communication and transport services, hotels and restaurants, and wholesale and retail trading. The industrial sector is experiencing growth with the construction of roads, railways, dams, parks, and housing.[5] Because the government dominates these industries, it is now one of the largest employers in Ethiopia. With very few corporations available (and therefore a small job market with limited options), most citizens work as federal employees or construction laborers. While some do work in private businesses, such as small-to-medium-sized shops and markets, these brick-and-mortar stores typically only need 3 to 10 employees to function, and they tend to pay less than the government, making them an unreliable source of income for most.

Prior generations followed a traditional career path. Most were hired by the government before even finishing high school, and they remained in the same position until retirement. That was, and continues to be, life for the majority of workers: Either find a government job or work in agriculture, perform the same tasks for more than three decades, raise children off of the salary, and wait for retirement. This just barely pays the bills and, not to mention, stifles innovation. Very few break out of this mold, fewer work in the private sector, and even fewer start businesses for themselves.

Of the few entrepreneurs who operate in Ethiopia, most work within the manufacturing sector, supplying basic metals and materials for construction and agricultural products for exportation. Most of their CEOs are in their 50s or 60s, or they are young adults who have inherited a generational business from their parents. While many of these companies *do* employ thousands of workers, they do not fit the criteria for new, entrepreneurial startups that boost the economy. With the factory and agricultural areas already being so well-established, entrepreneurial opportunities must expand outward and be represented across every industry, especially newer industries such as tech, in order to fuel the economy further.

With agriculture, manufacturing, and government positions being the most common and visible options, many young people entering the job market feel disempowered and trapped into choosing between limited, unpurposeful careers. These university graduates do not envision a predictable life in the same federal role, especially as these positions become more selective, competitive, and scarce. Nor do they wish to go back to farming with their families as most come from rural areas but attend university with much higher ambitions for sustainable incomes. After living in the city for four or five years and working hard to earn specialized degrees pertaining to their passions, the majority of graduates cannot see themselves back on a farm, performing manual labor oftentimes without the use of machines or tractors. Doing so would feel like a waste of their degrees, time, and dreams— though, with the absence of available jobs in the city, this is what many must resort to.

Young people want new experiences, new opportunities. Even if they do secure a city job, the repetitive nature of the work bores them once they have been trained, often draining them of the ambition that prompted them to attend college in the first place. In response, the majority of the workforce looks elsewhere for employment—in most cases, outside of Ethiopia and to the US and Europe—which represses the Ethiopian economy by undermining its number-one advantage: its large youth population.

Unlike prior generations, graduates now seek a wide breadth of opportunities across all industries: technology, politics, real estate, education, art, healthcare, sciences (psychology, sociology, biology, psychics), mathematics, history—and finally, *business*, which has the power to touch every industry imaginable. But for several reasons, entrepreneurship is not seen as a viable choice, despite business and engineering degrees being the top two certifications earned in Ethiopia. In other countries, examples of successful entrepreneurs, such as Steve Jobs, Jeff Bezos, and Bill Gates, permeate the media and become household names, but Ethiopian entrepreneurs— or even simply Ethiopian professionals with wealth—are few and far between. The successful business people who do exist hardly inspire and excite the newer generations with visionary ideas and fast-moving startups, instead falling into more traditional industries and following set paths. The country's recent history with financial corruption also makes it difficult to trust any wealth accumulated from prosperous industries and companies, instead promoting a culture of shortcuts rather than persistence.

Without role models—a precedent of ordinary people who have overcome conflict to build something bigger than themselves—it can be difficult to find the willpower to work hard and reach your fullest potential. You begin to think that even if you put everything you have into your passions, nothing will change for you or your family. If no one has done it before, or even executed something similar, success seems almost impossible. Ethiopia still has many "firsts" to reach. The problem becomes when people see these "firsts" as impossibilities, not opportunities, as the road to achieving them has never been paved.

Yet, I believe that most people do not realize how fulfilling entrepreneurship would be for them, how it would solve many problems in the lives of young people and in their communities. More Ethiopians have entrepreneurial mindsets than they know. Instead of considering a self-owned business, though, they find fault with themselves, their government, and/or their culture, thinking, "I become bored too easily and do not have a purpose in life. My government does not provide me with enough job opportunities, and all the ones available to me seem pointless. The people around me do not work as hard and yet make the same wages, so I should either forget my dreams or move away. After all, I have never seen someone make a real, lasting difference in my society."

All of these thoughts are signs of an entrepreneurial mindset. If you become bored too easily, you likely need an ever-evolving challenge, one that makes a real impact and shows tangible results for all your efforts. If you are having trouble finding a job that resonates with you, then *create* your dream job. Better yet, create it and then pass the opportunity on to others like you who have the same vision. Finally, if you feel like you constantly go the extra mile but are not rewarded, consider channeling that energy and vigor into something *you* control. Do not wait around for someone else to do it first because, by that point, it will be too late for you to stand out, seize the market, and make a lasting name for yourself.

So, be creative. Be different. Be daring.

Be your own role model.

Be first.

The Common Good

After WWII, Emperor Haile Selassie attempted to carry out economic reforms but was met with famine and economic hardship, the result of which was a 1974 coup by the Derg which led to a time of immense political and economic turmoil. In addition to the Ethiopian Civil War, nationalization and collectivization led to an economic crisis that contributed to a 1980s famine and resulted in one million deaths. Hundreds of thousands fled the country to escape poverty and conflict.[6]

Though the Derg dissolved in 1991, its deeply rooted communist principles continue to influence Ethiopia's laws, government, and societal norms. Even a 1986 *Commentary* article critiques the Derg's power over commonly held beliefs:

> Communism appeals to the Dergue for the same reason it has appealed to the radicalized elites of other Third World countries: It seems to be a means of transforming a backward society while bypassing the normal stages of development. [. . .] Borrowing a page from the experience of other Communist societies, the Dergue has placed its hopes and energies on instilling in the younger generation socialist values and a hatred for all things American.[7]

The EPRDF may have instituted a new constitution and parliamentary republic in 1994, but 30 years is hardly enough time for a country to shake communist dogma. Many civilians continue to distrust wealth, private businesses, and capitalist ideas, also largely due to the amount of corruption still present in political spaces. Businesses still encounter corruption in tax collection, customs clearance, and land administration— and many government contracts, especially in the energy, telecommunications, and construction sectors, are widely considered corrupt. The government also administers all land in Ethiopia, meaning that land is public property and therefore cannot be mortgaged. The government retains the right to take and redistribute land for "the common good," i.e., for farmland, industrial zones, and infrastructure, but allegations of corruption in land allocation have been prevalent as well.

Although Prime Minister Abiy punished existing corruption on a large scale (firing many corrupt civil servants) and works with the Federal Ethics and Anti-Corruption Commission to prevent future fraudulency, political malfeasance continues to infiltrate many areas of life, affecting the public's opinion of private businesses and also the ability to launch, build, and maintain a business at all.[8] The country's communist history continues to pose a threat to startups, the economy, and overall entrepreneurial morale. In particular, the amount of government-owned enterprises introduces a level of control that stifles new businesses before their ideas can reach execution.

Perhaps no other organization exemplifies this better than Ethiopia Investment Holding (EIH), the strategic investment arm of the government established in December 2021.[9] With over $150 billion USD in assets, EIH is the largest sovereign wealth fund in Africa. It employs about a quarter of a million employees and encompasses almost 30 state-owned enterprises across diverse industries, including manufacturing, construction, energy, finance, hospitality, and transportation.[10] Many of the companies under its umbrella once had intentions to be privatized, but years later, EIH still maintains control of significant economic players. Now, private business professionals look forward to the day that EIH starts becoming smaller and smaller, making room for non-public entities to operate and profit.

As of 2024, the most notable EIH-owned organizations are Ethiopian Airlines, the Commercial Bank of Ethiopia, Ethiopian Shipping and Logistics, and Ethio Telecom.

➤ Ethiopian Airlines

Founded in 1945 by Emperor Selassie, Ethiopian Airlines (shortened to "Ethiopian") is the multi-award-winning national airline of Ethiopia and one of Africa's leading carriers. Currently, Ethiopian has a fleet of more than 146 modern aircraft and serves 136 international passenger and cargo destinations.[11] As one of Ethiopia's major industries and an economic pillar, the airline has generated profit during almost every year of its existence.

Despite Ethiopian's success as the continent's largest airline and one of Ethiopia's largest employers, the nation has still failed to create a well-developed private sector in the aviation industry. Even the CEO of Ethiopian, Mesfin Tasew Bekele, advocated for opening the aviation market as doing so would "increase competition and reduce the costs for travelers amid rising demand for flying."

Although Prime Minister Abiy Ahmed planned to fulfill this vision and lead airline privatization efforts upon his inauguration in 2018, these plans were suspended in 2020. According to Finance Minister Ahmed Shide, Ethiopian generated so much revenue that privatizing it would harm, rather than help, the economy, stating that "maintaining the current capacity of Ethiopian Airlines is more beneficial to the economy."[12]

➤ The Commercial Bank of Ethiopia

Approximately 31 banks operate in all of Ethiopia, serving its population of 115 million people with 11,281 branches. The sector includes a central bank (the National Bank of

Ethiopia or NBE), a state-owned development bank (the Development Bank of Ethiopia or DBE), a government-owned commercial bank (the Commercial Bank of Ethiopia or CBE), and 29 private banks.[13] In 2022, the state-owned NBE reported deposits equivalent to over $30 billion and loans equivalent to over $25 billion, and the CBE had the highest number of branches with 1,444 locations.[14] The following year, the CBE continued to hold the largest share of bank deposits at 48.7%, followed by Awash Bank (8.4%) and Bank of Abyssinia (7.3%).[15]

With no foreign banks yet in the country (although plans are in place to invite foreign entities into the banking sector), the total capital generated by 29 private banks only superseded the state-owned banks by 6% in 2022:

- **Private banks**: 53%
- **Commercial Banks of Ethiopia**: 30%
- **Development Bank of Ethiopia:** 17%[16]

Also, due to the domination of state-owned enterprises, it was not allowed, by law, to set up an investment bank in Ethiopia until early 2024. As such, no investment banks currently exist in the country, and commercial banks can only offer businesses limited funding options. The director general of the Ethiopian Capital Market Authority, Brook Taye, describes this as "the biggest bottleneck in the Ethiopian economy," as businesses are currently paying 25% interest on commercial bank funding and have to provide collateral worth 70% of the loan's value. The demand for capital-raising services only continues to increase as more private businesses attempt to open and seek financing.[17]

Ethiopian Shipping and Logistics

Ethiopian Shipping and Logistics (ESL) is a consolidation of four formerly independent enterprises: Ethiopian Shipping Lines Share Company, Ethiopian Maritime and Transit Service Enterprise, Dry Port Enterprise, and Comet Transport Share Company.[18] The merger was intended to be a solution for the poor performance of each enterprise, with the goal being that together, they could streamline the logistics sector. However, a 2019 article by *The Africa Report* reveals that "despite posting substantial profits—$111 million in 2016–2017—ESL has been plagued with inefficiencies," with two-thirds of companies reporting ESL services to be poor:

> Firms complain in particular about its monopoly of imports by sea. Manufacturers and exporters regularly experience delayed deliveries, as [ESL] has only a limited number of vessels capable of calling at all ports of origin. Some studies have indicated that [ESL's] monopoly may increase shipping costs by 30–50%. Many Ethiopian companies simply establish sister companies in Djibouti in order to avoid using it.[19]

These firms are correct. ESL *does* have a known monopoly on transit logistic services, causing it to suffer from long queues of shipments and a lack of available containers. This is why one of Prime Minister Abiy Ahmend's flagship policy reforms aimed to liberalize and privatize the logistics sector and why, in 2021, the government attempted to alleviate the monopoly by allowing five private operators to be involved in moving cargo shipments.

Transport and logistics officials claimed the decision would encourage competition, improve efficiency, and cut back on foreign currency expenditures for shipping. But in direct contrast, other experts disagree and criticize the move, stating, "They`ve simply expanded the multimodal operator from one to five, hardly a liberalisation move."[20]

Unfortunately, the undertaking to privatize the logistics sector has appeared more difficult to achieve than hoped as years pass without much movement.[21] As of 2024, ESL continues to dominate the industry while maintaining ineffective operational practices, serving as a prime example of a sector that would be thoroughly reformed via privatization.

Ethio Telecom

Emperor Menelik II introduced telecommunications service to Ethiopia in 1894, approving the construction of the telephone line from Harar to Addis Ababa. The telecom service was first called the "Central Administration of Telephone and Telegraph System of Ethiopia" under Menelik II but was later changed in 1975 by the Derg to the "Provisional Military Government of Socialist Ethiopia Telecommunication Services." After a restructuring and several name changes, the modern-day Ethio Telecom was put into operation on November 29, 2010.[22]

From 2019 to 2020, Ethio Telecom collected a total of 47.7 billion birr ($1.4 billion USD) in revenue, a 31.4% increase from the previous year. The rise is attributed to network expansion, customer experience enhancement, significant tariff reductions, and newly discounted products.

Ethio Telecom's success makes it a valuable resource, one that Prime Minister Abiy sees as a golden ticket for opening up the economy. Plans to liberalize the telecom sector have been underway since 2018, and although

Kenya-based Safaricom became the first private investor to receive an operating license in 2021 (with an offer of $850 million and a promise to invest $8 billion USD in Ethiopia over the next decade), the government continues to look for another investor to purchase the second license available. Setbacks, delays, and war have limited investor interest, especially as a nearly two-year war in northern Tigray interrupted all progress. But, as a ceasefire agreement was signed on November 2, 2022, the search for external telecom investors resumed.[23] On February 9, 2023, the Ministry of Finance released an official Request for Proposal (RFP) to invite proposals from all interested parties. A bigger portion of Ethio Telecom is now on sale, the stake increasing from 40% to 45%.

As the Ministry of Finance once said in a statement, "Over the last decade, Ethiopia has become one of the fastest-growing economies in Africa. Its young population, high gross domestic product growth rate, and increased private sector investment offer valuable growth opportunities. Further, low tele density in Ethiopia highlights the huge untapped potential in Ethiopia's telecommunication sector."[24]

Choose Ethiopia

Take a moment to think: What global Ethiopian brands can you name? What businesses even have the name "Ethiopia" in them, apart from Ethiopian Airlines? I am sure, after listing a number of businesses in your head, none immediately come to mind.

Also consider that Ethiopia is one of the only countries in the world without a McDonalds. No Starbucks, no KFC, no Taco Bell—and beyond fast food, no highly recognizable global brands to speak of either.

While Microsoft, Google, IBM, Oracle, and other large corporations have offices in other parts of Africa, the closed nature of the Ethiopian market ultimately deters external investors. Even though Ethiopia has a population three times larger than nations such as Kenya, its laws, policies, and economic uncertainties discourage an open market. This is why very few brands are well-known across Ethiopia and why none expand out of the country, even if they succeed in the local market. It also explains why other African companies enter Ethiopian markets, attempting to take some market share and compete with Ethiopian companies for multimillion-dollar projects. Yet, Ethiopian companies do not branch out and try to compete in neighboring markets in return, instead sticking to the Derg-ian ideal of staying within their own borders.

I mention this not to say how great the presence of foreign companies would be when increasing the quality of life in Ethiopia, but to demonstrate that they would bring necessary competition to markets. Rather than allow them to enter markets and dominate the cash flow, effectively crushing existing local businesses, Ethiopia must ask foreign companies to collaborate and establish preconditions for their entry. For example, India once put in a policy that mandated joint ventures; if a large corporation wished to open, it had to partner with and uplift smaller, local companies.[25] Similarly, Dubai placed a 49% shareholding limit in United Arab Emirates (UAE) companies within permitted sectors and only allowed foreign companies to own 100% of entities in "free zones."[26] This mimics the Philippines's 1991 Foreign Investment Act that states at least 60% of any foreign business should be owned by a Filipino citizen while the rest can be owned by an international investor.[27]

No matter the solution, business owners can no longer close their doors in the pursuit of "getting by." They must open up, be ready for competition, find inefficiencies in their processes, and hire past two to three employees, instead growing bigger and stronger to validate their business model amid more established corporations. Once the majority of businesses graduate from that smaller level and pursue more capital and corporate governance, not only will they create a more sustainable foundation for themselves, but they will also help create a better, more streamlined society as a whole.

Amid these challenges of government ownership, the path to an open, more prosperous, and more competitive economy lies in wait—an opportunity the government is now trying to seize, both for the benefit of the economy and small businesses hoping to grow into something larger than ever before possible. Ethiopia is shifting into an unprecedented time of economic transformation, exemplified by all the progress already being made:

- The EPRDF released a statement in 2018 that claimed the government would wholly or partially transfer its shares in state-owned railways, hotels, parks, and manufacturing companies to private investors.[28]

- While the telecom sector was once completely owned by the government, the introduction of Safaricom paves the way for a private industry, already bringing improvements to competition, connectivity, and infrastructure.

- Licenses will soon be issued to allow foreign banks into the country.

- In 2024, the Ethiopian Civil Aviation Authority issued a directive that enabled private investors, regional governments, and city administrations to engage in the development and administration of not only airports but air transport services, aviation academies, and aerospace manufacturing.[29]

Despite this immense opportunity, some concern still hinders privatization, a common thought being that if Ethiopia opens its economy, its money will funnel out of the country, not in. Almost like leaving the back door of your house open, many think privatization is a gateway to theft from other nations. Despite this, I continue to see the benefits, not the dangers, as more sustainable. The commitment will require dedication from both sides: The government will need to provide the field to play in, but then Ethiopia needs to run free and take advantage of the opportunity, making money and growing the economy.

Believing that people will only take money out of the country prescribes to that antiquated communist mentality, which says to limit wealth and safeguard what little you do have. My way of thinking is that even if someone has a nice home in Dubai or a large property in the US, Ethiopia can still be a place where they return, where they call home. If Ethiopia becomes an enabling environment, why would someone move their family across the world, especially if their mother, father, and/or relatives live in Ethiopia as well?

By creating a peaceful and sustainable economic environment, the mentality shifts from one of control ("You cannot find other opportunities outside of the country") to one of freedom and choice ("You can spend your money wherever and however you want, but Ethiopia has become so attractive that why would you spend it anywhere else?").

In other words, do not *force* people to choose Ethiopia.

Give them a reason to *want* to choose Ethiopia, again and again.

CHAPTER FOUR

Expedite Systems

A struggling software developer trying to launch a new product, a young Samrawit Fikru worked late into the night. Tired and frustrated, she grew hopeless, working hard at the office even though the National Lottery had rejected her company's idea of an SMS lottery system. Her stress only compounded when, in the early hours of the morning, Samrawit would finally leave the office and walk down the empty, dark streets attempting to hail a cab. Flagging down a cab was difficult; feeling *safe* in a cab was even rarer.

Samrawit began surveying others about their experiences, only to find many people had similar stories. Identifying a real market gap, Samrawit and Hybrid Design PLC, the company she established with three friends, began working on RIDE. At first, RIDE used SMS to help users hail a taxi. Customers would text their location to 8200, and the system would connect the customer with a nearby cab driver, who would either accept or reject. Upon acceptance, RIDE provided the customer's phone number to the driver, so the two could negotiate a price.

RIDE evolved as new smartphone capabilities expanded, making way for the RIDE app. Users only had to dial 8294 or download the app to find a safe, reliable taxi near them. Hybrid Design also updated its internet-based services and its call center and grew from 3 employees to 52. Today, more than 50,000 people have downloaded the RIDE app.[1] It is the largest taxi-hailing service in the nation with more than 5,000 registered drivers.

As part of an early press initiative, Samrawit once called a journalist to explain RIDE's mission. After detailing how the app worked, the journalist paused and then asked, "Oh, so it's like Uber?"

Samrawit took a moment to think but then responded, "What is Uber?"[2]

Though both RIDE and Uber are ridesharing companies, Uber was born out of the need for *efficiency*, seeing as it was once very difficult to find a ride on the busy streets of San Francisco. RIDE, in direct contrast, was born out of the need for *safety* and *availability*.

Apart from typical startup struggles, including driver recruitment and turnover, product-market fit, and software development, RIDE also experienced hostile competition. Code-1 operators (public transport service providers) once "blocked RIDE vehicles, damaged property, and even assaulted drivers," protesting that RIDE drivers were stealing their jobs. This only caused the government to see RIDE as a threat rather than an economic benefit.[3]

In 2018, the Addis Ababa Transport Authority attempted to ban rental transport service providers joining RIDE, stating that cars with commercial (Code-3) license plates could not be part of the platform. It also demanded that RIDE had to obtain licenses from the Transport Bureau before starting operations. The majority of RIDE's 900 licensed rental service providers were forced to cease operations, and most vehicles with RIDE windshield or bumper stickers were fined.

"They have no legal right to operate in the transport sector nor does RIDE have a legal entity to operate routes. We have checked the legality of RIDE, and we have learned that it only has a license for software and application development. [It does not] have a transport operator's license," argued the general manager of the Addis Ababa Transport Authority.

These complaints did not stop Samrawit, however. She spoke to Takele Uma, deputy mayor of Addis Ababa, to discuss the constraints. Takele expressed his sympathy, recognizing that RIDE plays an important role in hiring young people and filling a vital public service. He also stated that transportation as a whole should be left to the private sector.[4]

A month later, the Addis Ababa Transport Authority repealed its objection, and RIDE was free to continue its upward mobility. So far, no authority has successfully placed in-depth regulations on the taxi-hailing industry due to the lack of a legal framework, but many believe that with the emergence of more than 30 similar ridesharing businesses, which were inspired by RIDE's success, the industry must be formalized.[5]

Today, RIDE is one of the most recognizable private brands in Ethiopia, and with more than 300 full-time employees, 90% of whom are female, the company continues to grow alongside developing legislation and partner with multibillion-dollar corporations to help expand the Ethiopian gig economy.[6] Yet, in Ethiopia, great success does not protect businesses from setbacks.

Despite not having seen a computer before the age of 17, Samrawit Fikru became one of the nation's, and the continent's, top entrepreneurs. But even she recognizes one of the biggest threats to entrepreneurship in Ethiopia: red tape.

Waste Your Week

All Ethiopian business leaders can attest: One minor bureaucratic issue can waste your week. In Ethiopia, public service offices do not meet the efficiency standards of other countries and, therefore, require mass amounts of time, often asking individuals (including non-entrepreneurs) to fill out physical forms in person and then return to these offices several days in a row. Even a simple process, such as receiving the title for a new car or a new house, takes days and involves a surplus of unnecessary steps. In many instances, I have personally stood in line at a federal office for hours, only to be turned away and told to come back the next day. This exasperating culture of difficulty contradicts the ideal goal of a government: to make life easier for its citizens. The same sentiment only proves truer for entrepreneurs, who must deal with the same inefficiencies as average citizens *in addition to* the ineffective systems required for business ownership.

Despite Ethiopia's 2019 Growth and Transformation Plan (GTP), which placed entrepreneurship at the center of economic advancement, aspiring business owners still face several significant challenges when establishing businesses, let alone refining and scaling them.[7] With a shortage of experienced mentors and investors, novice business leaders—through no fault of their own—often cannot find the guidance, resources, or information necessary to even apply for a business license. Not only do the lack of incubators, accelerators, tax incentives, and financing opportunities inhibit the startup ecosystem, but the absence of education in all matters of business registration deter startups. In Ethiopia, a stifling amount of bureaucracy is the first thing many encounter when attempting to open a business. Notably, it is also often bureaucracy that causes many to give up or, in some cases, not try at all.

The process of opening a business in Ethiopia entails a maddening cycle: Visit an office in person, fill out paperwork, wait, visit another office in person, fill out more paperwork, wait again, and so on and so forth. Few resources, online or otherwise, detail each necessary step, and even if you know how to fill them out, the required forms take hours to complete and submit. This office-paperwork-wait cycle continues not for days but for *weeks*. According to the 2019 World Bank's *Doing Business* Report, it takes an average of 32 days to start a business in Ethiopia. Compare this to the approximately four days it takes in the US and UK and even the 23 days reported by Kenya.[8]

Many entrepreneurs avoid this time-consuming paperwork by hiring business consultants and lawyers to help register their companies. Finding this representation is often the first step to establishing a company, for an experienced legal consultant can provide information and guidance that may not be readily available otherwise, including particular legal obligations for specific industries. Although this is the standard in the majority of established business environments, Ethiopian business culture does not value legal representation. In fact, many grow concerned when I mention IE Networks's legal department, a dedicated unit that only assists in legal consultation and decision-making.

"Why do you need a legal department?" some ask. "Do you have conflicts with the court?"

Contrary to the social perception of why people employ lawyers (where business owners only hire legal aid when they encounter litigation), I do not employ a legal team due to an urgent need. Rather, I see the legal department as a preventative measure. By having a lawyer review essential documents, provide advice, and create contracts from the beginning of a client relationship, IE Networks protects itself, its employees, and its clients. The risk of going to court reduces, rather than increases, which makes legal representation a vital component of any business.

Unfortunately, not many Ethiopian business consultants or lawyers have been available in the past, and in the present day, few options exist. Even though legal representation can be necessary, especially in the beginning stages of registering a business, the majority of Ethiopian lawyers do not specialize in business practices, instead engaging in criminal justice. For instance, the legal team at IE Networks entered the company with degrees in general law and then later gained the necessary knowledge of contract laws, labor laws, and international business laws through online courses and training.

Despite the benefits of legal assistance, I recognize that this is not an option for many beginning entrepreneurs who operate on limited funds and time. For such founders, a more customary route—one that can be done independently—exists: applying for a business license, receiving a tax identification number, and learning how to remain legally compliant. The road may be paved with bureaucratic red tape, but those who can see past initial challenges and into a better future—one where they own a company, drive a mission, and bolster their community—can persevere through any inconvenience, independently or with help.

Stable, Strong, and Streamlined

Even if you intend to hire a lawyer for assistance, you will benefit from understanding the ins and outs of authenticating a business in Ethiopia. By law, businesses can be established as a sole proprietorship, private limited company, share company, branch of a foreign company, public enterprise, or cooperative society. Ensure you choose the best classification for your industry and the desired growth level of your business, but know that whichever classification you choose, the business registration process remains nearly identical. The number of steps involved can seem lengthy and complex, so I have distilled the process into five key stages.

1. **Establish a company name at the Ministry of Trade and Regional Integration (MoTRI).**

   When you ask to set up a company at the MoTRI, the office officials will run your business's name through the system to ensure it meets requirements and is not already in use by another company. Though this may seem straightforward, finding a name for your business may pose a significant challenge. Even IE Networks went through more than six names to arrive at its current title. At first, I browsed through different options and presented several to the MoTRI (called the Ministry of Industry at the time). The office, having very strict naming requirements, declined each idea, claiming that most of the names were already taken, not permitted, or too descriptive. I was so busy at the time that my wife went on my behalf to sort this out— again, only to hear that it wasn't possible to find a name.

   My wife and I wasted weeks on this one task that could have been simplified through an online portal, where I could have typed potential names to check their availability and compliance. The inefficiency and tedious nature of having to return to the MoTRI office in person cost us time and, therefore, money. In addition, the lack of clear criteria for business names seemed endlessly frustrating. To approach a MoTRI officer with a list of names and be turned away each time, without being given notes on how to improve or what requirements to meet, felt like we kept hitting a brick wall before we could even start our business. What should have been an exciting time turned into an exhaustive dilemma.

The immediate setback could have tarnished my morale and dissuaded me from continuing to pursue my business license. After all, the beginning of a business, when you do not have much at stake, is the easiest time to quit. However, an ideal name soon presented itself. Since I had recently earned my CCIE certification, I decided to take out the letters *CC* and adopted the name IE, standing for Internetwork Expert. Finally, I had a name.

2. **Complete and submit a memorandum of association.**

   When I first established IE Networks, two documents (an article of association and an article of establishment) were required to request a business license. Now, however, the MoTRI has condensed these two documents into one: a memorandum of association. Once the MoTRI approves a name for your business, you will receive this document to fill out and return (unless you operate as a sole proprietor, in which case you will only need to provide your ID document for authenticating your company). The memorandum primarily asks for basic information: What is the objective of your business? Who are the shareholders, and what amount of equity do they own? Who are the executive officers, and what are their job titles?

Several questions on the form can be difficult to answer though, especially if the applicant is not familiar with business terminology. To further complicate matters, few resources exist for filling out these forms. Business consultants are few and far between in Ethiopia, and almost no templates or examples exist online. In my case, I was fortunate enough to have a friend who had gone through the process before, and I used his memorandum as reference to complete my own.

Not everyone has a friend with a business, however. For those who are intimidated by paperwork, forms, and documents and therefore hesitate to start their business, I encourage you to reach out to local business owners who have done it in the past. As with anything in business, a strong network of people who have been in your shoes will prove useful now and even more beneficial later. You will be surprised at how many people *want* to help you and see you succeed.

Remember, nothing is as difficult as simply starting.

3. **Apply for your tax identification number.**

Once you have obtained a business name and the MoTRI has approved your memorandum of association, you will also receive a trade registration certificate. With these three certifications in hand, you can visit the Ministry of Revenue to acquire a tax identification number, though the process may require scheduling a separate appointment and waiting several days. Once you have reached a certain revenue threshold, you will also have to register for a VAT tax certificate, a tax examined more thoroughly in chapter five.

Also consider that, before securing a trade registration certificate, you will be asked to supply an official rental agreement. In other words, the government will require you to supply a business location—one that cannot be your home address. This is a monumental barrier to entry for most startups, for by law, they must invest in rent. Therefore, startups always begin with operating costs. My hope is that, along with other technological focuses, the government officially discards this requirement (there was a recent mention of it by Prime Minister Abiy at a startup event) and begins to open the remote working space. Enabling individuals to launch online startups, potentially from their living room couches or home offices, would undeniably catalyze the private sector in a way never before seen in Ethiopian history. As with many areas of the country, if we can set technology as a priority, it will be a pillar.

4. **Receive a business license for each trade in which you intend to work.**

   With each of these certifications, you can now visit your local business registration office and obtain business licenses for each industry in which you work. The office will provide you with a list of hundreds of categories to choose from. For example, you can choose software development, electrical work, restaurant services, or a variety of retail stores. For every service you intend to offer, you will need a separate business license, all housed under the same company name.

   Also note that some categories require additional certifications and prerequisites. If you select an IT category, they may ask you to provide a competency certificate from the Ministry of Innovation and Technology. If you select a construction category, they may ask for a certificate from the Ministry of Construction. Specific categories even ask entrepreneurs to reach a certain number of employees before granting approval. This can often be a "chicken or egg" scenario: In order to obtain a business license in particular industries, you must first have employees, which implies you must run and operate a business without yet having a license.

Fortunately, several solutions exist for this scenario. In some instances, you can submit future employees' resumes as evidence of your business's credibility, but most commonly, business owners first start their company in a category that does not require employees. Then, as their company grows and they generate enough revenue to begin hiring employees, they apply for the secondary business license in a more desired category, now having met the requirements. Of course, this means only established entrepreneurs can launch businesses in particular sectors. For beginners, they will have to validate their concept as credible and sustainable before entering more complex industries.

5. **Begin running your business while ensuring you maintain your various licenses and certifications over time.**

Congratulations! After obtaining all necessary business licenses, you have a legally registered business and are free to operate, hire employees, and solicit customers. However, while the initial challenge of opening your business has ended, you will still need to invest great effort into maintaining your licenses and certifications.

The most substantial upkeep involves your business licenses themselves, which must be renewed at the beginning of every fiscal year. Secondarily, you will also need to declare your taxes, which, again, I cover in chapter five with more detail. The most important factor to consider, though, is that depending on your company's size, you will either need to file taxes every three months or every month.

More information about the Ministry of Trade and Regional Integration can be found at https://motri.gov.et/en.

Compared to 16 years ago when I started IE Networks, the process of business establishment has seen great progress. The only viable, long-term solution to streamlining these processes even further and building a foundation on which all startups can flourish will require technology—a now central focus of the government. When Prime Minister Abiy came to power, he stated that one of his biggest priorities was making business easier, with the intention of streamlining federal processes, introducing automation, and making resources more accessible. In 2020, Abiy made true on his promise by enacting a digital transformation strategy, which "aims to harness technology to drive economic growth, citizen engagement, and improved quality of life."[9] In the past, Ethiopia has faced great connectivity and technological setbacks, with its economy enduring a $100 million USD loss in 2020 due to an internet shutdown and another $145.8 million USD loss in 2022 for intermittent connectivity and internet blockage. Digital services, especially international businesses, rely on dependable internet access, and if the government hopes to ease entrepreneurial bureaucratic processes (such as business license applications and tax reports), internet freedom and innovation must become priorities.

Examples of how to build stable, strong, and streamlined government processes exist all around us. If the government can implement well-tested, secure tools to expedite systems, the quality of life in Ethiopia will drastically improve. By starting with simple changes, such as introducing online business license applications or online portals for submitting documents, we will see how small progress makes a huge impact. Then, if we take it to the next level—if we can identify discrepancies in how our country runs and find better ways to make operations faster, more convenient, and more understandable—all of Ethiopia will run like a computer, making even the most mundane of everyday tasks easier.

CHAPTER FIVE

The Tax Burden

In the early stages of IE Networks, I was fortunate. As a consultant, I had enough revenue to make a profit, pay employees a competitive rate, and scale my business with few setbacks. However, even in a time of sustained growth, IE Networks faced an increased capital requirement—partially due to the extra taxation required by customs at the airport.

With few fundraising opportunities, I approached a friend for a personal loan. In one month, I used the funds to free my items from customs, deliver products to a customer, and receive payment, which I then used to pay back the personal loan. With the loan repaid within the established deadline, the lending processes should have ended without any conflict.

Although, when looking through bank statements, tax authorities saw the loan deposited in my bank account. The loan, though paid back as shown in the statements, was seen as "income." The authorities believed that I was hiding a source of revenue from the government and, as a result, charged a 30% tax on the full loan amount. When I pointed out the discrepancy, tax officials refused to acknowledge the money as a loan, did not consider the proof of repayment, and demanded the 30%. Even with this proof and with a lawyer, I would still have to pay 50% of the claim if I wanted to take the matter to court and go through the appeal process.[1]

Such extensive obstacles and tax burdens—some of the most grievous barriers to opening a business in Ethiopia—force founders to either disband their startups or move to a neighboring country where taxation does not chokehold revenue. Rather than encouraging small businesses to grow, the government increases tax obligations to the point of extortion. Then, when challenging the laws, business owners will often be told to obey an "internal directive" and are shrugged off without any logical discussion.

As you may imagine, there is no area of Ethiopia more rife with corruption and inefficiency. Continual tax audits breed distrust between companies and their government, a corrupt dichotomy that goes both ways.

On one side, tax fraud is rampant in Ethiopia, and business owners in Addis Ababa openly admit to engaging in large-scale tax evasion. Paying taxes in a law-abiding manner often means spending several days at the tax office, resulting in lost time and revenue. Evading taxes is sometimes the only way a company can continue to provide services because doing so allows entrepreneurs to offer more competitive prices to customers, make larger and much-needed profits, and spend more time working on the business.

Many times in the past, I have submitted business receipts to the government, only to be told that the store or business from which I purchased goods does not have a legitimate tax ID number. In other words, the business did not legally register itself as an entity and instead falsified an ID. With no way to tell which companies are registered and which ones are committing fraud, IE Networks, and other businesses doing work in an ethical and compliant manner, bear the burden.

The government invalidates the ethical buyer's expenses to receive more taxes—but then does not take action against the fraudulent seller.

A study by the London School of Economics and Political Science states that in 2020, Ethiopia had a low tax-to-GDP ratio of 6.2%. The most common methods of tax evasion include under-declaring profits and over-declaring expenses, under-declaring the quantity and quality of goods the company imports, and not declaring VAT taxes.

"Small and medium-sized business owners in Addis Ababa see paying taxes as an inefficient allocation of resources and tax evasion as an economically rational decision," the study states. "Business owners say that tax officials lack the technical capacity and goodwill to execute their jobs and are more interested in collecting bribes than serving citizens."[2]

Similar sources reaffirm that in 2018, 89.8% of taxpayers did not comply with the law's existing tax structure, a direct response to corruption on the federal side.[3] Most citizens do not believe their taxes are being used to finance public services for the betterment of the country; instead, the perception is that the money goes to politicians and civil servants. In accordance with this, bribes are commonplace, either in an effort to reduce the amount of taxes owed or to cover up discovered tax fraud. It is also not unusual for tax officials to openly demand bribes at the tax office, in front of other citizens and office authorities.

Though taxpayers do admit to substantial acts of tax evasion, they also describe the tax authority as "the [scariest] government office for the business community."[4] If caught, tax evaders can face prosecution and severe punishment, including jail sentences. The blatant and unapologetic lying, corruption, and fear create a perpetual cycle—one of negligence and missed opportunities for the country and its people.

The solution may be complex, needing time, focus, diligence, and upheaval, but a solution is paramount because no area of entrepreneurship poses more of an obstacle than the current tax regime. To eliminate such a deeply rooted barrier, we must first look at how it became so ingrained, what systems exist now, and methods for wide-scale improvement. Only then will we be able to create an inviting, empowering culture for businesses in Ethiopia, something that will bolster the country in all possible areas.

Spend Money, Make Money

The legislation surrounding business licenses and tax codes stemmed from the old commercial code, developed in the 1950s and 1960s. When the government began updating this code in 2002, however, it did not bring the code to the appropriate modern level nor implement it accordingly.

Under the governance of Prime Minister Meles Zenawi, Ethiopia introduced an unprecedented taxation system:

> Efforts to improve tax collection and stimulate investment included a modernized legal framework, more favorable terms for businesses, the issuance of taxpayer identification numbers (TINs) to all businesses and individual taxpayers in urban areas, the establishment of a value-added tax (VAT) to replace the existing sales tax, the collection of new excise duties on luxury imports, the introduction of mandatory income tax withholding by employers, and the establishment of a self-assessment system to enable taxpayers to complete their own declarations rather than having all payments calculated by tax officials. By 2006, however, the country's tax-to-GDP ratio not only had failed to grow but also had

declined to 10.7% from 11.8% in 2002 despite three years of GDP growth in excess of 10% annually.[5]

The same taxation system established by Meles exists today with little modification. The inefficiency and lack of online services waste valuable time and resources. To this day, despite having a chief financial officer and many accountants on the IE Networks team, I must still carry out menial tasks, such as going to the tax office in person. Rather than giving tax breaks or tax returns for businesses, the government instead "squeezes" businesses for taxes, sometimes doubling or tripling the average amount.

The most relevant and problematic of taxes include:

> **Value-Added Tax (VAT)**

In 2003, value-added tax (VAT) replaced sales tax as a tax on the consumption of goods and services. The tax was introduced as a solution to several problems and aimed to:

- minimize tax avoidance,
- enhance economic growth and the importation of goods,
- improve the relationship between domestic production and government revenue, and
- increase savings and investments.[6]

When companies reach a certain revenue milestone, they must register for the VAT in addition to their tax ID. The VAT requires businesses to place a 15% additional charge on every offering, which will be paid to the government. Not much has changed since the tax's establishment as VAT still applies to nearly all products and services, with the exception of airline travel.

One interesting detail here is the concept of a "tax refund." Unlike in America, where citizens file for tax returns in the spring, Ethiopia does not have an individual tax refund system. Only businesses can request tax refunds, of which there are two types: withholding and VAT. In both scenarios, companies can request a tax return if the government withholds more money from the business than the business withholds from its suppliers. Likewise, the company may have to pay the government back if it withholds too much from its suppliers. A withholding tax return requires businesses to wait until the end of the fiscal year to file a tax return, but a VAT return can be filed after three months.

Unfortunately, requesting any type of tax return typically elicits an automatic audit. As previously mentioned, tax authorities use audits as a way of finding "secrets" the company is "hiding from the government." This means that when businesses request tax refunds, what usually happens is that, rather than giving them a return, the government instead asks them for *more* money, often double or triple the amount of what the return would have been.

The result is that businesses are discouraged from filing tax returns, knowing that it is an open invitation for corruption.

Withholding Tax

Corporations face 2% withholding taxes, which apply to payments for supply of goods and provision of services to a resident (in addition to 3% withholding taxes when importing goods, as shown below). The supply of goods must be worth 10,000 ETB or more, and the provision of services must be worth 3,000 ETB or more for the tax to apply. Another requirement is that the supplier in the transaction must provide a business license and a valid tax identification number. Without these items, the payment is subject to a withholding tax of 30%, a significant increase from 2%.[7]

> ## Import Tax

There are five different aforementioned taxes that apply to Ethiopian imports: customs duty (0%–35%), excise tax (10%–100%), VAT (15%), surtax (10%), and withholding tax (3%). The percentage of tax depends on a variety of factors such as the type of import and amount already paid to other taxes. The government of Ethiopia implemented these taxes in an effort to increase the competitiveness of the domestic producers, set low taxes for raw materials not found in Ethiopia, and align its own tariffs with that of the World Customs Organization.[8]

For IE Networks, we import many items from third-party companies, such as Cisco and Dell, and the import taxes are always extremely high. More than that, many tax officers assume that we are trying to cheat the tax system when we tell them how much the import is worth, so they charge more than necessary, claiming that we under-invoiced the item. This results in long fights with the tax officers and halts our projects because we are unable to receive our imported goods until the matter is resolved.

The government also recently introduced a new import tax called "social welfare," an initiative first started in 2022 as a response to political instability, the COVID-19 pandemic, and rising global commodity prices. The levy places a 3% tax on items that importers bring into the country. Exempt imports include fertilizers, petroleum products, mass transport vehicles, and capital goods.[9]

The problem with this, besides the addition of yet another tax, is how it was communicated to the public. IE

Networks was not informed of the tax's existence nor were we charged the additional 3% with each import. Three years later, the tax authority calculated all the "missed" 3% charges from the past years. We only discovered this when we received a letter from the Customs Commission, stating that we had millions of birr worth of unpaid taxes, based on old imports from years ago. As IE Networks had already completed those projects and delivered the products to customers, we could not go back to customers and say, "You did not pay the 3% social welfare tax three years ago, so you must pay us now with interest."

With the proper communication and implementation of this law, IE Networks could have incorporated it into our cost structure. Instead, the "surprise" introduction of taxes cost businesses like ours millions.

Surtax

Ethiopia introduced surtaxes during the Eritrean–Ethiopian War, which spanned from 1998 to 2000. However, even though the conflict with Eritrea has been over for more than two decades, the surtaxes remain. Today, all goods imported into Ethiopia, with very few exceptions, are still subject to a 10% surtax.

Excise Tax

When Ethiopia implemented excise taxes, the idea was to discourage the importation of harmful substances, such as alcohol and tobacco. Now, excise tax is charged on any excisable goods manufactured in Ethiopia by a licensed manufacturer, excisable goods imported into Ethiopia, and excisable services supplied in Ethiopia by a licensed person. Generally, the rates of excise duty range from 5% to 500%, the 500% applying to goods such as old motor vehicles.

> ## Technical Services Tax

Many additional tax laws continue to limit and prohibit rather than encourage, one of which includes the technical services tax. In an environment with a great need for well-trained, experienced talent, businesses must provide perks and growth opportunities to employees in order to retain them. Yet, taxation laws dissuade such training initiatives. For example, IE Networks pays for certification training for its employees as I hope to pass on the same opportunities I received when attaining the CCIE certification, knowing what previously unattainable doors it opened for me. With no options existing within Ethiopia, IE Networks pays for an international service through a third-party company. Despite this being a direct transaction from one company to another, the Ethiopian government charges an additional 15% fee for the training service. Yet again, even though companies try to do right by empowering and educating their employees, both for the betterment of their business culture and the entire country's workforce, a penalty is placed upon them. A punishment rather than an incentive.

> ## Business Tax

Perhaps the most exhaustive tax requirement is the business tax, or profit tax. Every year, businesses must submit expenses, costs, and revenue and then pay a 30% tax on all profits. And although companies may not face any tax challenges during the first years of their startup, it is only a matter of time before they encounter an audit.

Every few years, tax authorities will audit a company with the assumption that executives are not reporting some revenue. The perception seems to be that businesses pocket all revenue and that operating costs do not factor into profit. For example, if a company reports $10 million in revenue but $5 million in total profits, tax officials will attempt to discard as many expenses as possible, even if those expenses are legitimate costs needed to sustain the company. Therefore, the officials may ask the company to pay taxes on the total revenue of $10 million rather than the $5 million profit. And while any business owner would be proud to claim a 100% profit margin, that is not a realistic standard. Businesses must spend money—on rent, on salaries, on business events, on travel—to make money.

Hustle Culture

As stated, companies of a certain size must declare VAT taxes. For smaller qualifying businesses, this is only required every three months, but larger qualifying companies must declare VAT taxes, pensions, and withholdings every month. Even the companies that have not generated any revenue for the period must declare zero revenue or face a steep penalty.

The frequent filing of taxes acts as a severe overhead cost to new businesses, especially if they must file every month. Hiring an accountant can be a major expense, but independently taking on that responsibility requires time and involves the risk of completing the forms incorrectly, which could result in legal complications.

This challenge is compounded by the fact that many companies wishing to report losses cannot do so. The impression is that if a company declares a loss, it is really hiding revenue from the government. While the tax office may accept a declaration of loss in the first year of business (even if it will likely send a warning letter in response), it will not accept the loss for another year. Instead, tax officials try to find a way to invalidate necessary expenses. Say a business makes $90,000 in revenue but spends $100,000 in operating costs. Rather than allowing the business to report a loss, the tax office will list each expense and rule out a number of them, stating that some expenses (though essential) were frivolous or unneeded. Put bluntly, it can feel like the tax office is hustling you.

Businesses pay taxes from profits, not losses. Developing the necessary infrastructure to generate revenue requires time, much more than two years. With the lack of external funding and investment options, companies are essentially being penalized for not executing a perfectly bootstrapped business plan within a short time frame—an unattainable feat for most. As a result, Ethiopia's strict taxation laws intimidate new business owners, and when forced to pay without first making a profit, founders feel demotivated rather than encouraged to grow.

For these reasons, businesses hesitate to scale, for growing to a certain size assigns them the title of "wealthy" and invites more tax collectors to collect profits that the business needs to survive. Companies do not want to be visible as this increases attention from tax authorities, making scaling nearly impossible. In fact, many companies create five, six, seven additional smaller companies when one business grows too large. Rather than grow into one large, successful company, many founders will instead set up a new business with a separate license, wanting to stay small and out of the government's field of view. The majority also complete informal transactions rather than formal, documented transactions to avoid the government's attention and the hefty taxes that would diminish profits. The reliance on under-the-table, cash transactions stifles economic cash flow, the consequences of which are increased risk of tax fraud and higher inflation rates.

In addition to irrational tax requirements, the government continues to ask companies and business owners to contribute to federal programs. A founder of any size company may receive countless letters asking for donations so that the government can build a new park or host an important political meeting—initiatives that taxes should already be funding. Again, the lingering communist mindset greatly influences how the government perceives and approaches businesses. Instead of supporting industrial growth, the view is that all well-established businesses have a surplus of money that should be funneled back into the economy and should *directly* sponsor federal projects.

The core problem, then, is that there is no benefit to becoming bigger from a tax point of view. In some other countries, tax incentives are plentiful, and business owners are proud to take advantage. In contrast, Ethiopian business owners are told to feel ashamed of using such resources. Even Kenya is undergoing major tax reforms with the 2023 Finance Act, which aims to remove the VAT on exported services, pay all tax refund claims within six months, and remove the tax on unrealized gains on employee-allocated shares for startup companies.[10] Kenya also plans to introduce paramount tax incentives and deductions across various sectors, including agriculture, IT, telecommunications, and construction.[11]

Fortunately, Prime Minister Abiy has made reducing tax evasion a priority, noting that despite the country's history of authoritarianism, enforcing tax compliance has been a key challenge that restricts the government's ability to implement new policies and spearhead new projects. As part of this effort, the prime minister invited the top 500 Ethiopian taxpayers to an award ceremony in 2024, where he handed out trophies. I was honored to attend such a ceremony and express my view on taxation, only to be met with understanding and reassurance. The prime minister expressed that his plans for improving tax relations in Ethiopia will extend far beyond galas and medals. He hopes to extend the possibilities of taxation for entrepreneurs to support a healthy, flourishing private sector, building out existing tax exemptions to include more industries and promote new, innovative startups as well as tax incentives for foreign investors in order to attract foreign investment.[12]

In order for an empowering business environment to come to fruition in Ethiopia, the conversation must ultimately shift to culture. The solution is not as simple as introducing new tax policies aimed at specific sectors, though this is certainly a critical part of the whole. Rather, the government must move toward a future of trust—trust in its citizens, its processes, and its officials to do the right thing and uphold justice when faced with corruption.

The dilemma with taxation impacts more than surface-level legislation and how much someone or an organization pays. It extends deep into the core of the country, consisting of disbelief in the government, mistreatment of citizens, and incompetency on both sides. This rotted core must be extracted, replaced, and then cultivated, the effects of which would do more than change a simple taxation law—it would change the entire relationship between the government, businesses, and citizens.

CHAPTER SIX
Accessible Financing

At the beginning of IE Networks, before even establishing a public office, I entered a project bid concerning servers and storage. A business issues a project bid when it needs a solution from a third-party company and invites other companies to apply for the job. Although I was successfully awarded the bid, the project terms stated that the customer would only pay 30% of the amount upfront and then pay the remainder once IE Networks delivered the agreed-upon solutions. There was also a stipulation that the customer would pay the advance payment if I could provide an equivalent "guarantee amount" from the bank. Approaching the bank, however, I was told I could only secure a guarantee if I provided *collateral* worth the same amount.

Collateral refers to an asset, such as a house or vehicle, that is pledged as a security for a loan. If the borrower fails to repay the loan, then the lender, typically a bank, can seize the collateral. Therefore, IE Networks may have been awarded the bid and we may have had the technical skills to execute the project, but as a medium-sized business, we did not have enough assets to leverage as collateral at the time.

As my family did not have much to put up either, I asked my wife's family and my friends, some of whom pledged their vehicles and other assets. Finally, the bank gave us the guarantee, and we presented it to the customer and received the advance payment . . . except the advance was not enough. We needed a loan as well.

This was an exceptionally stressful time for IE Networks. Previously, when I was asked to build a system, my knowledge and my time were the only prerequisites, but this being our first large project, it required a cash payment to import goods from abroad. Although, in this instance, we found a way to secure the cash, provide the items to the customer, and repay the loan, we encountered many other similar scenarios in the future.

As a company grows, the financial requirements also increase. Once a company hits certain milestones and reaches a large enough size, personal assets or the assets generously given by loved ones will no longer suffice. Especially in certain industries, no vehicle or house is worth the amount needed to expand a multimillion-dollar business. Despite this, there is no bank willing to help without adequate collateral. And unfortunately, banks are one of the only reliable sources of external financing in Ethiopia.

Small-to-medium-sized businesses account for approximately 70% of urban jobs in Ethiopia. Nevertheless, it is these same businesses that struggle the most when financing their operations. Bank loans may be the most prominent and feasible option, but even with only one pathway to follow, finding and securing external capital is anything but streamlined. Entrepreneurs must either bootstrap with existing wealth, ask for investments from friends and/or family members, or apply for loans from financial institutions, which involve high interest rates, long processing times, severe collateral requirements, and limited bank locations. This is why some sources state that only 350,000 people (0.28% of the population) have access to loans from banks.[1] Others claim that in a country with a population of over 100 million, the total number of bank loans disbursed in Ethiopia is only 250,000.[2] Furthermore, the public sector is often prioritized, with only 26% of loans being directed toward the private sector in 2021.[3]

Ethiopia's banking sector includes the National Bank of Ethiopia (NBE), the Development Bank of Ethiopia (DBE), the Commercial Bank of Ethiopia (CBE), and 29 private banks. In 2023, private banks accounted for 63.8% of total capital while state-owned banks accounted for 36.2%.[4] These private banks, of which there are too few to serve the large population, offer identical services: basic savings accounts, checking accounts, and loans. Without specialized products, such as investment, mortgage, receivable financing, or payroll financing, they all operate in the same way with no *distinct* value added to the economy.

Ethiopian banks are also extremely risk-averse. Although IE Networks has operated for more than 16 years and has seen great success in profit and employee retention, it is still considered a startup in the eyes of the bank. New, small, or established, all companies (and individuals) adhere to the same collateral requirements. If an entrepreneur requests $5,000, then they must put up $5,000 worth of collateral. Likewise, if an entrepreneur needs a million dollars, they must do the same. Typically, no lending officer reviews a business model or a company's value; rather, the only question that holds influence is whether the borrower can put up a house, building, car, or other piece of property equal in value to the loan amount. Because 96% of bank account holders have less than 200,000 ETB (equivalent to about $1,803 USD per August 2024 conversion rates), such stringent rules surrounding collateral make loans an unfeasible option for most—yet they are seemingly the only avenue for financing in the country.[5]

The reliance on bank-provided funding creates a discouraging financial environment in Ethiopia. With limited venture capitalists, private equity firms, other investors, credit systems, or clients willing to pay businesses in a timely manner, startups have a difficult time even launching, let alone scaling.

IE Networks, for example, has more than 200 employees, has an industry tenure of more than 16 years, and has an annual revenue in millions of USD with profitability every year. Even so, I can say that we continue to struggle with finances.

As the scale of the company increases, so do financial obligations. IE Networks serves influential clientele, such as banks, universities, and government agencies. These organizations require millions of birr in project expenses, even before factoring in service charges. Such projects act as immense expenses to IE Networks, which should be offset by payment from the client. However, we have millions of birr in accounts receivable. Customers are not paying IE Networks on time, which puts the company in a deficit.

When it comes time to pay employee salaries, for example, we may not have adequate funds as we wait for customer payment. As a solution, we look to external funding to buy time and pay employees until the customer compensates us. Then, after delivering under such strenuous circumstances, the customer sometimes penalizes us for delayed delivery. Rather than understand the different challenges IE Networks went through to complete the project, the customer calculates the number of days the project was delayed and deducts the amount as "liquidated damages." As a result, the initial projected profit decreases.

Payment delays are painful, especially when working with a government institution, where accountability is rare. Even if we draft and sign legal documents that mandate on-time payment, government officials seem to laugh and say, "Go to court and see who wins." And they are right; if we took them to court, the process would be too long to make it worth the effort, and the money still would not come. This is partially why financing has been the most pervasive challenge for IE Networks.

Even though I am proud that we have never defaulted on a loan, I also recognize that companies with 16 years of proven experience and a distinguished reputation should not face these financial problems at all. The formula inherent to the financial sector, however, keeps companies in this uphill battle position by demanding collateral or denying funds.

In other countries, a company that performs well is typically *offered* financial services or can pitch investors to receive additional resources. Many opportunities for credit exist, in addition to accelerator programs and startup financing organizations. But in Ethiopia, the process is likened to begging. While success is certainly possible in the business climate, this is one challenge that can discourage aspiring entrepreneurs from the beginning. Financial struggles, more than any other obstacle, may be the number one reason why startups do not simply fail—in most cases, they do not even begin.

Fundraising in Ethiopia

Founder's Guide to Fundraising: Ethiopia by Nathnael Tsegaw and Michael Tomas acts as an informative guide and starting point when first beginning to fundraise. The publication covers every key step and nuance, including whether your startup would benefit from fundraising, all fundraising options in Ethiopia, and how to close deals with investors. One chart in particular, which has been adapted for the purposes of this book, is especially helpful in detailing the different rounds of fundraising:

Stage	Key characteristics	Deal range	Notable startups	Instrument	Funder
Pre-seed	Proof of concept	$15k–$300k	Chapa, EPhone, Garri Logistics	Grants, equity, debt, and crowdfunding	Accelerators and angel investors
Seed	MVP testing	$500k–$1m	RIDE, Arifpay, ZayRide	Equity	Venture capital and angels
Series A	Expansion to new markets	$1m–$5m	M-BIRR, HelloCash, Kifiya	Equity	Venture capital
Merger and acquisition	Expansion to new markets	$30m–$100m	Apposit	Equity, debt	Companies, corporates, startups

In addition to the most accessible option of banks, *Founder's Guide to Fundraising: Ethiopia* puts forth several institutions to solicit funding: accelerator programs, angel investors, venture capital funds, and government offices.[6] Each of these, as well as several others, are explored in depth below.

➢ **Digital Lending**

Several digital lending platforms are now available to grant loans without collateral or extensive paperwork requirements. Some include Michu, a platform by the Cooperative Bank of Oromia with Kifiya Financial Technology, and Telebirr, which has a microloan service in partnership with Dashen Bank and the National Bank of Ethiopia.[7] According to the NBE, in the first nine months of the 2022/23 fiscal year, a total credit of more than 3.6 billion ETB has been provided through banks in partnership with Telebirr. This is four times more than the same period in the previous year, demonstrating the growth of the digital lending ecosystem. Such a system, if refined and well-implemented, has the potential to offer easier access to credit for borrowers and also enables lenders to reduce costs and reach more customers.[8]

To ensure these digital lending platforms reach maximum efficiency, a regulatory framework must be developed to protect consumers and lenders alike. Currently, Ethiopia does not have a strong credit scoring system. Many entrepreneurs, myself included, have foreign credit lines because other countries encourage the opening of credit cards. These systems do not require the account holder to be a citizen of the country and will often provide credit limits of thousands of dollars, set to grow over time if the holder proves responsible and diligent about repayment. Meanwhile, in Ethiopia, even attaining $1,000 in external funding can feel insurmountable.

➢ **Government Funding**

The DBE offers financing opportunities for designated industries. The recent focus has been to provide medium and long-term loans to "priority" businesses specializing in commercial agriculture, agro-processing, manufacturing, and mining and extractive industries.[9] After submitting a business proposal, these government-identified priorities then apply for financing. In order for the government to fulfill this inquiry, all domestic investors or borrowers must provide at least 25% of the total project cost, and the bank will finance the remaining 75%.[10] For example, if a company asked for a million dollars, then it must first have at least $250,000 to receive financing. Assuming the company meets the criteria, the bank then issues a loan with a low interest rate and long repayment period.

Because this loan option does not require collateral and only applies to government-identified priorities, it opens itself up to potential corruption. Yet, the more substantial problem is that the loan only helps a limited number of entrepreneurs, so very few people receive funding this way. Other industries also critical to any nation's survival and growth, including technology, do not yet see the same support.

For example, IE Networks applied for a DBE loan to finance a cloud infrastructure initiative in early 2024 and received a quick, albeit confused, response. No policy or directive is in place to accept IT projects. If I had a factory or farmland, the bank would have been able to finance specific machinery for me without any issue, but because I operate in the tech industry, the bank officials seemed perplexed at what I needed the funds for—a clear contradiction to Prime Minister Abiy's economic program that prioritizes digital transformation.

Months passed with no progress or movement since first requesting the loan. But seeing as I was fortunate enough to receive an invitation to an event with the prime minister in support of high taxpayers, I had the opportunity to bring this issue to Prime Minister Abiy's attention.

"Prime minister, sir," I addressed him, just one person in a sea of 500 other attendants, and I explained IE Networks's interest in a loan from the DBE. "I was told the bank does not offer IT financing."

The prime minister looked surprised. "Really?" he asked, looking to the governor of the NBE. "It doesn't? Why are we not supporting tech companies?" He turned back to me and nodded, promising that he'd bring it up in the next cabinet meeting for discussion.

IE Networks's vision of providing large-scale cloud services has been in development for more than 16 years. This mission only evolves as the most successful companies in the world move to cloud services such as Amazon Web Services (AWS) and Microsoft Azure, which offer a monthly or annual subscription service in order to house data. These offerings mean that companies and the government no longer need to invest millions of dollars in upfront capital for physical infrastructure and data centers, with extra benefits including streamlined sharing capabilities and more reliable data protections. While cloud sharing is undoubtedly the future, it is also very much the present as all major corporations have fully integrated cloud capabilities into their business models.

In 2022, two large-scale data centers were constructed in ICT Park. The first, completed by Wingu.Africa, is the country's first carrier-neutral and commercial data center and hosts up to 800 racks with 10MW of power.[11] The second, by Raxio, houses up to 800 racks and delivers 3MW of power.[12] Together, these data centers are capable of supplying thousands of servers, yet the government continues spending millions of birr on new facilities. The two centers in ICT Park remain mostly empty as a consequence.

Abiy Ahmed has issued directives to address this inefficiency, stating that companies and the government must take advantage of established data centers before constructing more. However, the data centers are only the first step. In order to function, they need tech companies to install and run the servers.

IE Networks is only one instance of a company that could use DBE funding to radically change the landscape of

Ethiopia. Increased cloud services would impact every area of the government by reducing expenses and improving overall functionality—if only banks would heighten their awareness of businesses outside manufacturing and agriculture. What other industries could make monumental impacts to the nation's way of life, given banks begin to understand the massive value these businesses could contribute to the country?

Domestic and Foreign Investors

Domestic development finance institutions (DFIs) and angel investors are currently the main contributors to Ethiopian startups, apart from banks or friends and family loans. Historically, Ethiopia has prohibited the involvement of foreign investors in the private sector. Consequently, very few foreign investors provide funding, and the ones who do tend to be angel investors, not institutions.[13] The policies surrounding these types of investors are antiquated. They assert minimum capital requirements for foreign investors, meaning restrictions prohibit certain sectors from accepting international funding or raising money from abroad. It is only since the inauguration of Prime Minister Abiy that the country has taken action to open the market and invite international parties. Now, doing so is viewed as a vital priority. Even Ethiopia's central bank, which defines the macro economy of the country, is attempting to open the banking sector to foreign players.

Other institutions have also been established to ease the process for investors, both foreign and domestic. Established in 1992, the Ethiopian Investment Commission (EIC) serves as a centralized location where investors can obtain visas, permits, and paperwork, thereby encouraging investments and the acquisition of business licenses. According to a 2021 report published by the US Department of State, the EIC holds several evolving responsibilities:

1. Promoting the country's investment opportunities
2. Issuing investment permits, business licenses, and construction permits
3. Issuing commercial registration certificates and renewals
4. Negotiating and signing bilateral investment agreements
5. Issuing work permits
6. Registering technology transfer agreements
7. Advising the government on policies to improve the investment climate[14]

In early 2024, the news agency Reuters reported that Ethiopia is set to open the country to foreign investment banks, catalyzed by the forthcoming Ethiopian Securities Exchange. The director general of the Ethiopian Capital Market Authority stated that the regulator is currently offering licenses to global and regional investment banks, securities brokers and dealers, and credit rating service providers who can help businesses list shares on the securities exchange and issue corporate debt.[15] Many international authorities have also expressed interest in Ethiopia. One includes the Ethiopian ambassador to Belarus, Shamebo Fitamo, who said that "investors of several European countries are very much desirous to engage in Ethiopia in various economic sectors." Another is the Ethiopian ambassador to Japan, Daba Debele, who stated that "initiatives are in place to entice Japanese investors to work in Ethiopia's mining, energy, and agriculture sectors."[16]

➤ Ethiopian Securities Exchange (ESX)

The Ethiopian Securities Exchange (ESX) is Ethiopia's first and only organized securities exchange. As such,

ESX will be the most significant and influential catalyst in supporting Ethiopia's private sector, specifically when concerning startup financing. The exchange's mission statement affirms it will "provide a modern, reliable, transparent, and efficient environment for securities trading in Ethiopia, through adaptation of modern exchange business operations, skill, technology, and trust."[17] The exchange also emphasizes a key concern: reliability. For a securities exchange to function, the system must be free of corruption and have proper regulations and laws in place to ensure all investments occur fairly and without scandal. Foreign investors will be entering the Ethiopian market with expectations of transparency and governance, potentially garnered from decades of investing in first-world environments. The ESX must meet these expectations head-on—for the benefit of both public and private participants.

In April 2024, the ESX had raised 1.5 billion birr. This transcends initial projections by 240%, both in terms of capital and in the interest shown by prospective investors. So far, these potential investors include FSD Africa, the Trade and Development Bank Group (TDB), and the Nigerian Exchange Group (NGX), alongside 16 domestic commercial banks, 12 insurance companies, and 17 other domestic investors.[18]

When the ESX launches, 50 companies are expected to list initially, though this number will grow as requirements for listing become less strict and more accessible over time.[19] Currently, the ESX has requirements that many businesses, despite their impressive size or revenue, cannot attain.

To list on the "main board" of the exchange, companies must have:

- an operating track record of at least three years (or have a partner who does),
- declared profits after tax at least once in the last three financial years,
- a total market capitalization of at least 500,000,000 ETB,
- a minimum of 15% of the total shares, and
- *a minimum of 300 shareholders.*

Recognizing that such a high number of shareholders is unattainable for most, the exchange alternatively allows companies to list on a "growth board," the requirements of which include having:

- an operating track record of at least two years (or have a partner who does),
- revenue increased by 20% annually in its last two years of operations,
- a total market capitalization of at least 100,000,000 ETB,
- a minimum of 10% of the total shares, and
- a minimum of 50 shareholders.[20]

While this is certainly *more* achievable for private businesses, the ESX will likely see more state-owned entities and high-revenue industries, such as banking, enter the exchange before others. Not as many shareholder opportunities exist for companies outside of these spheres, meaning they will have to play catch-up in the next few years to find investors, share equity, and reach the status of 50 shareholders in order to list. And though this may be frustrating for those who were looking forward to immediately listing upon its launch, it may be more beneficial to wait for the exchange to systematize, work out any initial inefficiencies, and mature overall before entering.

The ESX is set to launch in late 2024 or early 2025.[21] With it will come economic growth, financial inclusion, and more wealth as companies access better methods for raising capital and scaling their companies to support more employees, clients, and projects. Only one limiting factor stands in the way, the same factor that serves as a bottleneck in most areas of Ethiopian life and business—control.

The Definition of Risk

The mentality of control, a remnant of Ethiopia's past command economy, evokes ideas of theft and corruption. The current financial sector in Ethiopia does not adequately support businesses due to an absence of trust. This is only compounded by the country's lack of identification law.

In the US, citizens are given social security numbers. In Dubai, this is called an Emirates ID. However, in Ethiopia, millions lack identification. With no IDs or birth certificates issued by local governments, many cannot open bank accounts, access health insurance, receive cash transfers, or apply for government documents.[22] This also enables the forgery of documents such as passports and driver's licenses.[23] Some individuals own driver's licenses from multiple regions, all with different spellings of their names, thereby allowing them to open several bank accounts under various identities. Ethiopia does not even use a home address system, so all mail must be sent and received through PO boxes. This issue falls on banks, which cannot use addresses as a reliable way to identify their customers. These ineffective systems do not hold borrowers accountable or give banks the means to collect on debts; they only breed more fraud and distrust alike.

A solution to this was introduced in December 2023, but like most solutions, it will take years to implement fully. Fayda, the country's new digital ID system, is a unique 12-digit identification number issued by NIDP (National ID Program). Fayda collects both demographic data (name, birth date, gender, nationality, and address) and biometric data (fingerprint, iris, and face photographs) to deliver a Fayda Identification Number (FIN). NIDP intends to issue digital IDs to over 70 million citizens by the end of 2025. According to its website, "The program will be utilizing a variety of set strategies for enrollment, authentication, technology, stakeholder engagement, communications, and other range of important strategies put in place to achieve its ambitious enrollment targets."[24]

In addition to the FIN installment, other changes, such as the ESX, promise to ease the task of financing, albeit with time. One change involves the upcoming Startup Act, which establishes a startup fund, incentives for investors, more inclusion of foreign investors, and tax breaks. The act also solves a key problem, put forth by the increase in remote work, in that it will remove the requirement to obtain a business license before starting operations.[25]

Bringing alternate financing options to Ethiopia will result in new ways to finance business ideas and negate current collateral requirements, which serve as one of the greatest barriers to entry for any aspiring entrepreneur. Of course, laws that currently constrain the private sector will have to be revised in order to invite foreign investors and banks. These include laws concerning credit, startup financing, and investment options, such as private equity firms and venture capitalists.

But for now, as we work to improve fundraising capabilities and make entrepreneurship more accessible to all, financial risk means something very different in Ethiopia than it does in other countries.

Despite these deeply rooted challenges, my goal is to inspire future entrepreneurs to make big leaps and pursue unprecedented achievements. The country has always needed the service of these individuals, and I would argue it needs them now more than ever. The present day is the best time to finally put groundbreaking ideas into action. But as much as this is true and as much as Ethiopia and its people will benefit from new innovations, startups, entrepreneurs, and all of their aspirations—I also want to speak in favor of practicality.

Prioritize security. Guarantee food on the table, healthcare, and overall well-being. In America or Europe, if a business idea fails, the founder can still find work in their niche to support themselves, albeit with a chip on their shoulder. But in Ethiopia, failure for some could lead to much more dire consequences. In a nation with little financial support, a reliable source of income is so vital that naivete could lead to debt, repossession, financial instability, or any number of insurmountable fiscal problems. Instead of jumping feet first into a venture that will require millions of dollars in funding to execute, an entrepreneur can always test their idea through a "side hustle" or a freelance career to begin. Sometimes, the best course of action involves not a *fast* pace but the *right* pace for the circumstances.

Remember, you must survive before you can succeed.

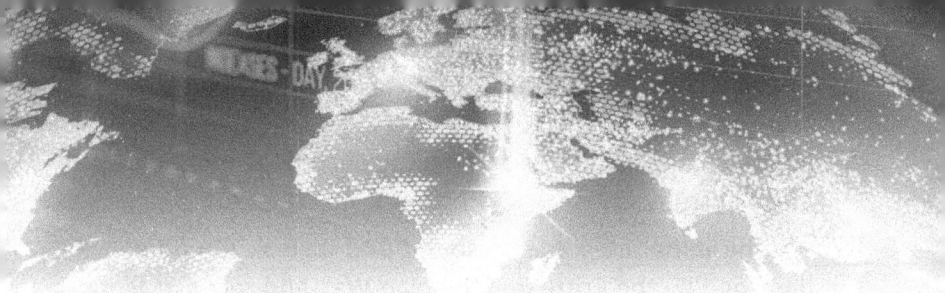

CHAPTER SEVEN

Invest in Learning

Taking office in 1995, Prime Minister Meles Zenawi adopted his own version of a "democratic developmental state," a model originated by South Korea and Taiwan that encouraged a strong state-led economy. He intended to mix the communist mentality with the economic direction of capitalism, with plans to move to a private economy over time as Ethiopia's needs evolved. That intention, however, was lost as government officials took power and did not wish to relinquish it in favor of private business.

Meles focused the country around infrastructure: new hospitals, bridges, roads, schools, etc. With that came a focus on technical needs. Who would design and construct these large-scale installments? Ethiopia needed technicians, doctors, and engineers. In response, the Ministry of Education launched a higher education policy in 2008: 70% of university students would be engineering and natural science students, and the remaining 30% would study humanities and social sciences.[1] The plan was to reach an annual intake of 212,000 students in engineering and 66,000 in natural sciences by the end of the 2013–2014 school year.[2] Again, said Meles, as the economy developed, this rule would evolve as well, and

Ethiopian universities could begin to encourage more diverse areas of study.

The initial idea seems sound and logical. Ethiopia was damaged by the Eritrean–Ethiopian War, and reconstruction was much needed. But historically, when concerning economic plans in Ethiopia, there are massive inefficiencies and unnecessary expenses. Resources were wasted, and projects were either delayed or never delivered. Government officials wastefully spent money and fell into corruption, so the education system, in addition to various other sectors, stagnated.

Today, the Ministry of Education perpetuates old habits and builds schools without proper infrastructure, leading to a lack of laboratories, libraries, and professors. In 2000, only two universities existed in the country, but by 2015, the government had constructed 29 more and planned to build another 11 in just two years.[3] Post-graduate enrollment also skyrocketed from 7,355 in 2007 to 40,287 in 2014. Likewise, the number of undergraduate students increased from 326,318 to 729,028.[4] Now, as of May 2024, Ethiopia has a total of 83 universities.[5]

A 2017 study found that this "rapid expansion of higher education was still challenged with educational service quality like absence of adequate classrooms, laboratories, dormitories, dining rooms, and other facilities." Similar studies argue that universities continue to struggle with budgets, staff shortages, and inadequate infrastructure.[6] Some even claim that those who have only recently graduated with BAs and MAs are becoming full-time professors right out of college.[7] In addition, a history of ethnic tensions and violence has caused students and their parents to apply only to universities located in states where their ethnic group is the majority. Public universities, in particular, have seen escalating ethnic tensions, which pose dangers to teachers, students, and property.[8] These challenges are only furthered by the impact of COVID-19, political conflict, recent environmental disasters, and a lack of academic freedom.

Graduates may hold degrees, but due to all of the reasons listed above and more, they leave college without understanding what their industries require. Even engineering students, who are the priority, do not learn from hands-on courses or laboratory experiments. Rather, their classes provide theoretical knowledge, worksheets, and tests. When these graduates enter the workforce, they have no experience to draw from, having never truly engineered, tested, and refined a product as part of a classroom setting.

Even if these students were perfectly skilled and prepared upon graduation, there are not enough jobs to accept them. Ethiopia's working-age population is currently estimated at 54.7 million—a number projected to grow by two million per year over the next decade. But despite improving education levels and the drive for industrialization, "youth are overrepresented in unpaid household labor, are more likely to be unemployed relative to older workers, are more likely to earn below the poverty line (for the few who actually earn wages), and are increasingly less likely to have access to land."[9] The unemployment rate saw a drastic increase in 2020, rising from 2.94% in 2019 to 4.02% after being below 2.8% for nearly a decade. However, in recent years, the rate has been on a steady decline once more, falling to 3.5% in 2023.[10]

The lack of entrepreneurship opportunities undoubtedly contributes to current job availability. As students only learn the "delivery" side of business and not the management side, they do not feel knowledgeable enough to open their own businesses and find work that way. With education being all delivery and no administration, the job market falls into a basic economic imbalance: all sandwich makers, no sandwich shops. When new companies do not open, an even more substantial job deficit is created, and graduates are forced to find low-paying labor jobs or jobs outside of their fields—or even outside of the country.

This culture originates from high school class schedules. In tenth grade, students typically choose between a career path in social sciences and natural sciences, the assumption being that intelligent students will choose STEM courses while low-scoring students will aspire toward the humanities. As business falls into the social science category, management or executive roles are devalued while "delivery" jobs (doctors, engineers, etc.) are applauded.

Even in organizations that can supply jobs for graduates, management training is often not prioritized, and delivery-level workers are promoted to managerial positions without the necessary expertise. Without educated leaders in position, basic tasks are not done at an appropriate speed or a higher quality. No trained and/or certified managers means that no one looks at everyday operations and asks, "How do we do this better?"

With inefficiency comes complacency. And complacency is the number-one killer of all businesses, cultures, and spirits.

Compare the Costs

If IE Networks plans to hire five new team members, 500 candidates will apply. Young people expect to graduate college and begin their careers, but not enough jobs are available, especially not jobs in specialized career paths, separate from traditional engineering and agricultural work. There are no longer enough government positions or professional opportunities. Yet, these graduates are college-educated and oftentimes the first in their families to attend university. They are ambitious and avid learners who wish to escape traditional means of living in Ethiopia. Most of them being from rural, low-income areas, many of their families cannot afford modernized machines such as tractors or combine harvesters and instead perform all duties through manual labor and handheld tools. The children of these farmers work hard to earn a diploma, many times experiencing city life for the first time, and do not wish to return to plowing fields.

Given this unique cultural circumstance, no matter how much filtering IE Networks does in learning about candidates' academic success, work ethic, and personality, almost all prospective applicants approach us with the same attitude: saying yes to every question and guaranteeing they can perform certain functions, even if they have no prior experience—anything to secure the opportunity and therefore an agriculture-free lifestyle.

Despite this enthusiasm, the most common method for recruitment is finding candidates via other companies, not hiring fresh graduates. When attempting to execute a project, companies will want candidates who are currently working on a similar project or have that very specific expertise from another business. But because finding professionals (let alone *specially trained* professionals) in the limited candidate pool is a daunting task, hiring managers will approach employees from other companies and offer them competitive salaries. The primary issue with this, apart from the obvious ramifications of employee poaching, is its impact on work culture. These new hires may be able to carry out that one project, but what happens when they are not a good culture fit as a whole? What happens when they must lead future initiatives after not having the time or experience to understand how the company or its people work?

Oftentimes, poached employees join an organization with disciplinary problems they learned from former employers. They may not come to work on time. They may not deliver projects by the deadline. In client-facing roles, they may raise their voices, talk casually, or speak to customers using language that is not congruent with their current company's values. Thus, the executives who hired them express frustration and lament the hiring decision . . . but they typically do not fire the individual. In fact, they continue to recruit employees using the same method as before, rather than giving more opportunities to existing employees or new graduates and intentionally building the culture of their organization from the ground up.

Most companies focus on the present day, not the future. With too much focus on the sales side, they fail to give the human side the attention it deserves. By only trying to survive, they do not allow themselves to later thrive. In order to be sustainable, businesses must take the time to step back and build foundational processes that will elevate them in the future, not simply grind away in the same ineffective routine, chasing sales day by day in an effort to stay afloat. Doing so will make the work seem tedious, unproductive, and endless for both the founder and their employees. Yet, when I suggest hiring junior employees with minimal experience, many leaders respond, "Why would I invest in someone I cannot use immediately? Why would I invest that time, commitment, and money?"

I always advise these leaders to compare the costs. The "poaching" method demands high initial, and sometimes long-term, investment. In order to hire a skilled candidate with prior experience, of whom there are very few in the job market, you must offer an expensive salary and benefits right from the start.

Then, when these candidates demonstrate poor performance, you must find someone else, continuing a cycle of inefficiency. Alternatively, if they do work well in the culture, you must alter your business model in order to continue compensating them at that high cost. Optimally, these hires would provide enough value to the company to cover their salaries. However, in some cases, such an operating cost could bleed a business.

By comparison, training junior employees from the beginning enables leaders to:

- build company loyalty,
- shape the company culture,
- influence how teams are constructed and how they collaborate, and
- ensure team members learn how to operate according to current company standards, not standards learned from prior experience.

This is why, in 2024, IE Networks launched the Graduate Trainee Program (GTP) to create a seamless transition for young people graduating and finding their place in the job market. For the first year of the program, we brought on 44 graduates from 16 universities in Ethiopia. By the end of the first two months, all of them had obtained international certifications and secured jobs, 37 of which were jobs at IE Networks. Because we had trained them ourselves, they were well-adapted to our culture and workplace practices before starting full-time. The success of the GTP was phenomenal just in the first year, and a replication of the program at other companies would only further boost our economy and propel our Ethiopian youth forward.

When IE Networks recruits today, we think about tomorrow. While reviewing resumes or interviewing candidates, we ask questions concerning potential projects in the future, even projects that will occur in a year or more. For us, hiring the perfect candidate is unrelated to past experience, earned degrees, or other hard skills most applicants can write on their resumes. Instead, we look for work ethic, perseverance, and a spark in the eye, something that tells us this person wants to be *here*—and wants to be better than they were yesterday.

A Pillar

In 2023, for the second consecutive year, more than 96% of students who participated in the national "high school leaving" examination did not pass. This means that hundreds of thousands of students did not qualify for university education.[11]

As almost all Ethiopian universities are state-owned, the government picks universities for high school graduates. Students submit their top three choices for university and their desired areas of study. Then, the government uses a system to assign students to schools, partially based on their grades. Top-scoring students may be granted their first pick while others could find themselves in schools unrelated to their passions. An aspiring electrical engineer could be assigned to a mathematics school and earn an irrelevant degree. A prospective medical student could be appointed to an agricultural sciences department, following a life path they did not choose. Those who are enrolled in their first choice are seen as "the lucky ones" who can pursue their interests—while others must adhere to a roadmap based on happenstance.

I was one of these lucky few. Across all seven of my "school leaving" examinations, I accomplished a rare feat: I made straight As. People who have done the same are very few and far between, which meant that when it came time to apply for university, the government assigned me my first pick. I chose Mekelle University, located in the Tigray region approximately 780 kilometers away from Addis Ababa. For the first time in my life, I traveled away from my hometown in the capital city to pursue an education in Mekelle, a much more remote landscape. A younger, more inexperienced version of myself wanted to see a different part of the country and put distance between me and my hometown, as most college students do. However, looking back, my time there was likened more to military camp than the proverbial "college experience."

By bus, the trip to Mekelle took three days, primarily due to the poor condition of the roads. Once there, I lived in a dormitory on campus with low-quality water—so hard that if you filled a glass with water, you could see yellow sediment fall to the bottom. By the end of my freshman year, after taking general courses for my first two semesters, I chose my department: electrical engineering. But at that time, this department was not established. The university offered majors in mechanical and industrial engineering but not electrical. Fortunately, I had the opportunity to join the first cohort in a brand-new electrical engineering department during my second year. However, as the area of study had just opened, it lacked the necessary professors and equipment. To try to fill the gaps, the college designated junior instructors and even brought in two international instructors from India and the US, but even then, the professors struggled to cover class requirements.

The most influential aspect of college was that people from all over the country attended classes with me. I experienced different cultures and met others with diverse backgrounds. We went to church and ate meals together, and although I had only been to two regions in Ethiopia at that time, I felt like I gained a deeper understanding of what other parts of the country were like. I studied at Mekelle University for a total of five years. While there, I learned quite a bit about myself but also about the people who would be entering the workforce alongside me. The majority did not enroll in school because of an interest or because they wished to discover a passion, something that would drive their professional choices and define their careers. They instead went to school because they sought an escape from laborious agricultural work, and while they did have areas of study, these concentrations were picked by the government on their behalf.

The consequence of this system is that the majority of people do not feel committed to their professions. College students push through four years of grueling, uninspired work, only to receive a valueless diploma and go back to school to earn another degree in something they care about or try to leverage the diploma they have in a disliked career path. Not only do these graduates enter the workforce without passion or drive, but they also do not receive the proper education to function in a professional environment. Many times, IE Networks has hired candidates only to discover they cannot write in English, compose a simple email, or properly communicate with others. They have earned a degree simply to do so, not because it fulfilled an inner purpose or provided foundational knowledge.

There is a massive burden on companies to train employees, and this training is usually complete not in one month or even six months but oftentimes a year or more. It is not enough for companies to provide entry-level training on processes and policies. Instead, they must begin with methodology, covering every aspect of the job and how to execute it. As an employer, IE Networks trains team members from scratch. In other words, we hire to train, not to work.

When fresh graduates or entry-level employees join IE Networks, they first begin with formal "classroom training," where they learn the basics of the job. In this stage, IE Networks establishes expectations, relays what the employee should expect from us, and provides targets. Then, the new hire follows a well-developed training curriculum, completing online courses that we created in-house as part of our learning management system. As soon as possible, IE Networks assigns new team members a coach for on-the-job training, in which the new hire shadows other employees with the intention of learning a specialized skill. The coach, a senior member of the team, helps the new employee adapt to the culture and understand processes.

During this time, the new hire spends half the day in training and the other half interacting with the team. We want them to feel like part of the company from the very beginning, so they spend a large amount of time in team meetings, doing minor tasks for other senior members, and learning team dynamics, all while assisting with projects, managing junior-level tasks, and carrying out online training. Once a new employee completes this, they can then be assigned to a project. Even if they do not have all the knowledge they need to execute the project perfectly, they always have a senior team member accompanying them throughout the entire process.

IE Networks also pays for certification training for every employee. After the new employee is assigned a project, for the next three months, we push them to work on their assigned project, take the certification course, and mimic their senior engineer. IE Networks *challenges* them to use their time to study, learn, and deliver. The tasks we assign encourage them to try hard, though they are always achievable with effort.

If they interact, ask questions, and hold high standards for themselves and their work, they build the necessary stamina, commitment, and career vision to flourish. Of course, we encounter new hires who do not want to be pushed. Some only want to do the minimum amount of work. These are people who are not in the right field or in the right place, and they will not benefit from what we have to offer. But these people are not the norm. More often than not, what we see is that these fresh graduates *crave* purpose. They want to see tangible results from their efforts and feel a sense of accomplishment. This is what builds self-worth and work ethic. It is what people strive for: to work hard at the beginning of their careers, knowing the inspiration they develop early on will translate into a successful, profitable path forward and beyond what they thought possible.

This investment in employee training comes at a significant cost to IE Networks. And although the qualification of these employees is vital to our operations, it is also the reason these same employees are either poached by other companies, which promise better salaries or additional benefits, or leave the country for better job opportunities. While we invest in employees expecting a return when they reach a certain skill level, that return is often not realized. Year after year, we must replace the senior employees and, again, start from scratch with another group.

Not every company puts such effort and funds into staff development, seeing as it requires investment and patience, and it's necessary for every new hire, not just once. But for me . . . I see this as the DNA of IE Networks. I want the backbone of Ethiopia, our young workforce, to see IE Networks as a career-defining opportunity, one only afforded to those with an appetite for a better future. A better future for them, of course, but also for their loved ones. And for the country as a whole.

At the time of Prime Minister Meles Zenawi's administration, Ethiopia struggled to regain footing after conflict. The country had to prioritize necessities such as food, water, shelter, healthcare, and basic infrastructure for its people. It was not meeting the first tier of Maslow's hierarchy of needs and therefore had to surpass that threshold before striving for other necessities, including specialized educational offerings. Thankfully, now that basic needs have been met, the education system can flourish as well.

This is just another way IE Networks makes a positive difference. For us, education is a pillar. Our staff members receive exposure to knowledge and experiences they never would have otherwise and are built into driven, efficient, and goal-hitting professionals. Whether they decide to take those skills to a higher level at IE Networks, another Ethiopian company, or abroad to a multinational corporation, I take pride that IE Networks helped them along their professional journey.

CHAPTER EIGHT
High-Performing Teams

When starting IE Networks, I was still working for Ethio Telecom in design and quality assurance, helping to execute multibillion-dollar projects as a technical consultant. I was also a freelancer in addition to this nine-to-five career, which meant my weekends and evenings were dedicated to various part-time jobs. I often worked for nine hours at the telecom and then another few hours on freelance assignments every day. Unsurprisingly, the work soon became overwhelming.

I built a good reputation for myself, and word had gotten out that I performed high-quality work. As a result, more prospects began requesting tech services. Even though I had the skills and knowledge to deliver projects, there were simply not enough hours in the day. With only one of me but several clients with pressing deadlines, the workload became impossible to execute on my own. Therefore, I began the process of hiring outside employment.

The first employee I hired was a former elementary school classmate. He was working as a network engineer for a university when I approached him. I needed someone to handle the basic tasks that consumed too much of my time and interfered with my ability to focus on more challenging senior-level work. He agreed, and thus, IE Networks's first employee joined the team. Though, from my perspective, I thought he would be the *only* employee rather than the *first*. But after him, the team naturally grew. Once I took on a new project, it only seemed logical to hire another person to help. Then, once I rented an office, we needed more than engineers; we had to hire janitorial services, an office manager, and an accountant. Departments began to form and grow as needed, and now, IE Networks has over 200 employees with plans for further expansion in the future.

What I learned from this was that while recruiting and hiring employees was difficult, the even bigger challenge was creating the internal structures and processes needed to facilitate a healthy work culture. Nonetheless, I had to do this in a business ecosystem that does not prioritize work culture or, in many cases, does not even acknowledge that a productive work culture is something worth having.

When beginning IE Networks as an independent freelance consultant, I only had responsibility for myself and my own productivity. My sole obligation was to manage my own time and abilities in order to deliver projects by the set deadlines. But when I brought on the first employee, those responsibilities multiplied: I now had to designate work for him and ensure he met those objectives. I did not know it at the time, but my first employee held an important role. He would lay a foundation for the entire work culture at IE Networks.

As the company grew, this friend had to serve as a role model for new employees. Each time someone joined the team, they looked to him as an example of how to manage time, clients, and quality of work. Growing to a size of five people and beyond, the culture of IE Networks began to evolve, whether or not I was present to influence it. Employees looked around and took note of everything from leadership expectations to the work ethic of coworkers. From their environment, they consciously or subconsciously learned how hard to work, how much discipline to have, and how to communicate with team members and clients.

There is only so much control a leader can have over this culture, for employees come from different professional backgrounds and have operated in a multitude of diverse environments, all of which had distinct job requirements. Some may be fresh graduates with no prior professional experience, unsure of how corporate workspaces are supposed to function. Others may have been in their industries for more than a decade and, as such, have grown unmotivated or apathetic to their profession. Each new hire brings a divergent experience that not only influences their performance but can impact how those around them operate as well. And while this is a universal fact about work culture, the challenges are only amplified when in Ethiopia—where there is no blueprint for how employees should engage with a business or vice versa.

Preconceived Notions

Yuval Noah Harari's book, *Sapiens*, details a brief history of humankind. In it, Noah Harari expresses a profound statement: Humankind's biggest achievements do not involve its discoveries but, rather, its ability to rally large numbers of people around a common endeavor. By my interpretation, I see this as the profound accomplishment of getting corporate-level employees, hundreds of thousands or even millions, to work together in support of one goal.[1]

Not many countries in the world can compare to Ethiopia's expansive involvement with the history of humankind. Yet, unlike in established capitalist countries, where corporate environments tend to have identical practices, Ethiopia does not have many reference points for how to manage (or "rally") people or structure hierarchies. In a country without a strong private sector, most businesses are small and informal, functioning with two or three employees. This poses a challenge for startups since a family-owned restaurant, for example, has much different cultural needs than an international tech company. High-revenue entities with intentions to scale must pay respects to delivery times, quality standards, proper human resource practices, employee performance reviews and training, and customer service, among many other considerations. The hardest part of this may seem like building everything from the ground up, but in reality, it is educating others to abandon preconceived notions of how businesses *tend* to operate in Ethiopia and instead aligning them with the *desired* culture.

For example, Ethiopian companies and their employees tend to operate via several *laissez-faire* mentalities:

➢ **Many companies in Ethiopia mix personal relationships with job responsibilities, valuing niceties and almost never firing or critiquing employees.**

Most work environments are so relaxed that proper PTO systems are not in place. If an employee would like to miss a day of work, they tell their supervisor that day instead of giving prior notice, and the supervisors grant them permission without any repercussions. In fact, some government employees also have part-time jobs and will leave their full-time federal jobs during the day to go work elsewhere. Even while at work, the attitude is often, "Why create deadlines? If I don't do something at work today, I can always do it tomorrow." Even Kenya's labor productivity is three to four times higher than that of Ethiopia, and Ethiopia's productivity level is far below those of Vietnam, Tanzania, Cambodia, and Myanmar.[2]

This overall lack of discipline leads to:

- high attrition rate,
- high absenteeism rate,
- no sense of urgency for work, and
- low motivation to complete quality, timely work.[3]

> **Very few trained, skilled professionals are available for hire in the current job market.**

As the quality of education is poor, students graduate from university without knowing basic administrative skills, such as writing a proper email or creating a slideshow presentation. Consequently, training in more advanced, technical skills is that much harder, for new hires are starting from scratch, not from an already-learned foundation of knowledge. These graduates' understanding of workplace etiquette and best practices is therefore also limited and even further distorted by the lack of good examples in Ethiopian culture.

> **Even senior professionals with established careers require fundamental training.**

Just like entry-level hires, those with 5 to 10 years of work experience only become productive members of the team in six months at the earliest. Both the age and work experience gap present several problems.

The first problem is that seasoned employees often do not wish to train under younger (yet more adept) employees who have not been in the field as long. However, these younger employees have experience with IE Networks, its specific operations, and its unique culture, so even if they have not been in the workforce for as many years, they have a lot of knowledge to offer any new hire. Yet, some senior members feel insulted when placed with a less experienced training coach, believing they are above learning the basics. The second challenge is that for many of the same reasons listed above, more experienced new hires feel entitled to a higher salary, whether or not they perform at the same level as others in the company.

Coming from a dissimilar work environment, many are resistant to change and hesitant to accept IE Networks's focus on creating a productive work culture. And I understand this frustration. Even after years in the same industry doing the same type of work, senior new hires find that no other company prioritizes productivity or upholds such strong values as we do. So, the main problem for these senior new hires is not *learning* new concepts; it is *unlearning* past habits.

➤ **Much of the common thought surrounding work stems from the government, for the majority of corporate workers in Ethiopia are, or have been, employed by the government.**

Government employees, even if they do come into the office, sit back and play on their phones. They go out for tea, come back an hour later, and then take their lunch breaks early, which go on for two hours at minimum. Out of the eight working hours in a day, federal employees typically work two or three . . . on *productive* days.

The Ethiopian government is notorious for missing deadlines. One day, the news will state a project will be completed in a year, and four years later, the same project will finally be done. The media will celebrate its completion, all without mentioning how the extra time needed hemorrhaged the initial budget for the project. Even if any progress is made, the extra time it takes ends up diminishing the country's economic value. This was exemplified in 2022 when the total public and publicly guaranteed debt accounted for half of the GDP.[4] No matter the scale or importance of the project, time seems to hold no value, yet no one is penalized for the delay or additional cost, despite the immense pressure this puts on the economy. The only exception seems to be Abiy Ahmed's personal projects when building parks, tourist destinations, and resorts, which are delivered on time and with high-quality results. Such productivity should be institutionalized and applied to all government undertakings.

➤ **Most leaders/managers adopt a "parental" role with subordinates.**

Though workers show a distinct lack of discipline, respect for superiors dominates the work culture in Ethiopia, with most businesses having strict hierarchies that enforce proper deference to those in leadership positions. The relationship between employees and employers plays an important role, for collaboration greatly depends on trust. Yet, as with a "parental" relationship, the leader tends to make decisions without input from subordinates and runs the company independently. Rather than allow subordinates to conduct work with the same independence, however, leaders typically micromanage, provide hands-on advice, solve problems, and directly mediate disputes, whether these disputes are due to personal or business reasons.

> **Most workers live in a comfort zone.**

Despite receiving low wages, the majority of Ethiopians accept their social statuses as an unchangeable part of their lives. They are comfortable, even when only being able to afford one or two meals a day.

This is perhaps the most concerning aspect of Ethiopia's negative work culture—that most people do not feel that by working hard, their lives may change. In other words, they are without hope for a better future and, therefore, without ambition.

In a population of 120 million people, there are few rich individuals. Those who do exist likely earned their money from government affiliations or family inheritances. The past has shown that people like this tend to be involved with some level of corruption. Thus, when the public does not know the source of a wealthy person's income, it automatically breeds distrust. The wealthy are not role models; they must be criminals. Without examples of successful Ethiopians who made a name for themselves *while* doing right by others, young people tend to think, "Why should I work hard? The only way to get ahead is to take a shortcut."

With such a predominant way of thinking, IE Networks faces great challenges when integrating new employees into our own culture, where we instill policies about being on time and delivering according to schedule—to the point where most new hires feel like they are stepping into an alien land.

The Quintessential Engineer

In my early years, I was the quintessential engineer: quiet and individualistic. A natural-born introvert, I did not engage with crowds or talk around the water cooler. I enjoyed technology, and all I envisioned for my future was Silicon Valley. To get there, I had to study, do my job, and deliver projects. No part of my professional life, I thought, mandated that I build relationships and learn to empower others toward the same levels of productivity. Little did I know that in a few short years, what started as a freelance career would grow into a full business with several employees, all of whom needed more than simple directions. They needed a leader.

I earned my undergraduate degree in engineering. I did not take a management course or a finance course. I had no idea where to start when it came to human resources, especially in Ethiopia's unsystematic business culture where nothing is standardized or "a given." Not many entrepreneurs were around to answer my questions or act as mentors, and little to no resources were available. It is because of this that I chose to pursue an MBA. I needed to know business, which meant I also needed to learn management.

In 2008, I applied and gained acceptance to Trident University International pursuing an MBA with a specific focus on IT management. Through the online program, I obtained foundational knowledge in basic human resource management, marketing, financing, and organizational culture. Before earning my MBA, I was just an engineer, a "techy." I did not know the first thing about the human side of business, yet I found I could make more of an impact with these learnings. Many engineers operate in Ethiopia, but how many also know how to rally people around an idea? How many know how to start a business at all? And how would the country change if more people *did* know?

Not everyone is cut out for leadership, but engineers, in particular, make great leaders. That is, if they can tap into the human side of business, not simply the delivery side. Engineering is about solving problems. The combination of the engineering side (building, tinkering, fixing) with the human side (empathy, vision, empowerment) is *powerful*. This is why I encourage all young, "techy" people, introverted or extroverted, to explore that other side of themselves. Bridging that gap may take effort and push them out of their comfort zones, but the chances of success become much greater.

I, myself, had to learn many lessons about leadership through diligent work and continuous education. After earning my MBA, I completed two Harvard Business School (HBS) courses, the Stanford Transformation Program (STP), and a Project Management Professional (PMP) certification. Much like my MBA, the first HBS course I attended covered the basics of business and launching a new venture—all information I already knew considering I'd been running IE Networks for nine years at that point. However, the course showed me a different perspective on the same concepts. This was Harvard, so an executive education program meant a six-day boot camp spent learning from (and making connections with) some of the greatest minds in the world. Then, I had the opportunity to learn even more in the second Harvard course on scaling ventures to a global level. In my opinion, this is when I truly shifted from a technical manager to an entrepreneurial leader.

As a technical manager, I assigned tasks, delivered projects according to deadlines and quality expectations, and managed my team and clients. But after my Harvard experience, I learned to be an entrepreneur who sees the bigger picture, that long-term vision. Rather than simply managing, I could lead, inspire, and motivate others. I also began to see my business as a global business. How could I—like the CEOs we studied who scaled companies such as Amazon, DropBox, and IBM into business titans—bring IE Networks to the same tier? How far could we go, now that I had the foresight to take us there?

The Stanford Transformation Program followed a similar pursuit as the second HBS course, though it only catered to African and Indian entrepreneurs. In addition, the one-year program was more for the entire company, not only the CEO, as it included the company's entire management team in developing a five-year growth strategy. This whole-team mentality is what I tried to convey to the interviewers when applying for the STP.

Looking at my resume, the interviewers asked a logical question: "You've earned your bachelor's degree, MBA, and completed two Harvard courses. Why are you applying to Stanford as well?"

"This is not just for me," I replied. "This is for my team."

In the Harvard courses, my classmates and I analyzed case studies from major corporations, but in the Stanford program, my actual team members and I worked together to form a strategic business plan for IE Networks. The course applied to real life in a more direct way and gave us a better path forward. It was like training, strategizing, and hiring a consultant all wrapped in a single undertaking. The program was so hands-on, in fact, that part of it even required a coach to meet with us in our homes.

IE Networks is now in the last year of the five-year strategy we built during the STP. Since then, we have achieved our set objectives year after year and look forward to setting new and more ambitious targets for the coming decade. This success can be attributed, firstly, to my dedicated team and, secondly, to numerous courses, books, advisors, and more than 16 years of industry experience, which have provided me numerous management insights. I have distilled these principles in the following pages, but the main key is performance management: breaking larger goals into smaller milestones, continuously evaluating, coaching the worst performers, and celebrating the best.

The first management book I ever read was *The One Minute Manager* by Kenneth Blanchard, PhD, and Spencer Johnson, MD. The book is a short, easy read yet is profound in teaching business owners how to simplify processes, boost productivity, and increase profits using three techniques: one-minute goals, one-minute praisings, and one-minute reprimands.

- **One-minute goals**: Setting (and then *communicating*) clear objectives is the most essential component to business success. Every team member must understand their role in achieving a set task, the expectations upon completion of that task, and *why* their responsibilities matter to the organization's larger purpose. Each goal should be so simple that anyone could read and comprehend it in a minute or less.

- **One-minute praisings**: Managers should praise employees when they catch them doing something right.

- **One-minute reprimands**: Managers also have a responsibility to reprimand employees when necessary. These reprimands should take the same amount of time as praise, never longer, and relate to the *work* that was done incorrectly, not the person themselves. Also, take care not to approach an employee with a reprimand unless the company already has a solution for it. What is the sense in telling someone they are doing something wrong if you cannot tell them how to do it right?

The principles set forth by *The One Minute Manager* directly led to the system IE Networks uses to establish, communicate, and fulfill goals. Upon reading the book, I went to our three employees at the time and assigned them each a weekly goal. This seemed simple enough, but in order to achieve the task in a week, they had to set daily goals for themselves. For the first time, my team members began creating checklists. While they were productive before, they suddenly became organized and, most importantly, *focused* on one objective with a clear deadline rather than several objectives with loose due dates. More than 14 years later, IE Networks is still powered by the holistic principles of *The One Minute Manager*, one of which is, "The best minute I spend is the one I invest in people."[5]

It was only when I read John Doerr's *Measure What Matters* that a more formalized structure took shape, beyond the basic ideas Blanchard and Johnson described. In the 1970s, John Doerr was an engineer at Intel, where, working under Andy Grove (described as "the greatest manager of his or any era"), Doerr learned a foolproof operations approach called Objectives and Key Results (OKRs). The system defined objectives as "what we seek to achieve" and key results as *how* those objectives will be attained. It emphasized the need for accurate data tracking and thorough, transparent communication so that everyone in the organization, from the CEO to the newest hire, recognized their responsibilities. Since being pioneered by Doerr, OKRs have helped tech giants, including Facebook, Amazon, and Google, achieve explosive growth with a central thought: "Ideas are easy. Execution is everything."[6]

OKRs are the backbone of IE Networks. Every quarter, we set ambitious yet measurable goals. Then, we break those goals into smaller, actionable milestones, the idea being that "if we can do *this*, *this*, and *this*, then we can achieve *this*."

The same system extends to every team member, all of whom have their own OKRs for the quarter. Everyone knows their objectives, which they can then divide into weekly goals, tasks, and checklists. In addition, team leads host weekly check-in meetings with team members to gauge progress and identify any problems, and on a monthly basis, the company reviews how OKRs are proceeding as a whole. Combining this with our regularly updated, well-documented standard operating procedures and training materials, we have created a process-oriented organization headed by a CEO who works *on* the business, not *in* it.

This open communication, delegation of authority, and structured system allows responsibility to be handed over, an experiment that IE Networks has coined "the CEO got hit by a bus." In other words, if the CEO suddenly passed away or went missing, would the company still be able to function? If not, what overly bureaucratic steps are in place taking up the CEO's time while, likewise, taking ownership from employees? What knowledge is only known by the CEO, and how can it be better dispersed? Basically, the CEO may be able to oversee things today due to their better understanding, but the question is whether someone else could take over if the CEO vanished.

What is most important here is how this system's design *supports* goal achievement. Every part of this approach revolves around goal-hitting, both for efficiency and as a way to inspire purpose. Rather than endlessly working toward nothing with no end in sight, employees aspire to achieve OKRs because they wish to influence a real, tangible change in the company—an impact that any employee can help bring to fruition. In African countries, where work can feel monotonous and tedious, and especially in Ethiopia, where most people do not work for jobs they feel passionate about, accomplishments (and rewards for those accomplishments) can change lives. For example, IE Networks encourages employees with incentives, announcements, and awards, including "Superstar of the Quarter" and "Employee of the Week," which applauds hard work on an individual basis. The purpose of our company extends much further than that, however. Our ultimate goal is our mission statement, an objective larger than any one person at IE Networks: "Change the life of Africa via a disciplined work culture and systems thinking."

We are a tech company, yet our mission statement says nothing about technology or innovation. Instead, it points to changing the whole of the continent, namely through how we conduct ourselves and serve as an efficient example for others to follow. To see this mission through, several core values, established by historically brilliant entrepreneurial minds, guide us.

- *Kaizen*: Small, achievable steps (or "continuous improvement") can lead to sustainable and enduring change.[7]
- **Extreme ownership**: Every person makes the company's mission their mission.[8]
- **Grit:** The secret to success is long-term passion and perseverance.[9]

Occasionally, I will be asked, "What was your number one success while building IE Networks?"

My response is always, "Building the culture."

I often think of Larry Page and Sergey Brin, who notoriously founded Google while working out of a garage. When asked how they built Google's culture, they responded by saying they simply tried to recreate the environment of that garage but on a larger scale. Following their example, I try to influence a culture that I too want to work in: one of commitment, passion, hard work, and also long-term thinking over short-term benefits.

For example, all companies in Ethiopia begin the day at 8:30 a.m. or later. But IE Networks starts at 7:30 a.m. I will admit that this is a consequence of me being an early riser who is happy to head into the office before the regular time. However, in Ethiopia, the majority of people may clock in at 8:30, but they also work on Saturdays. At IE Networks, it was important to me to give everyone that day off. So, pushing our start time up an hour enables everyone to enjoy their entire weekend however they see fit.

Those of us at IE Networks may wake up before anyone else, ready to work harder than anyone else, but that is ultimately so we can live freer lives—and inspire others to do the same.

CHAPTER NINE

Export African Talent

In 2019, over 1.3 million Filipinos were employed by business process outsourcing (BPO) companies—a number that was projected to grow by 8–10% each year. As of 2023, the BPO sector employs approximately 1.7 million Filipinos and contributes around 7–8% to the country's GDP. The growth can be attributed to the Philippines's skilled workforce and large English-speaking population with a literacy rate of over 97%. Due to these factors and more, the Philippines now holds between 10–15% of the global BPO market.[1]

The BPO industry has radically changed the way of life in the Philippines. GDP growth, export revenues, and investments transformed the economy but also introduced many new employment opportunities and changed how society functions. Similar to Ethiopia, the Philippines has a large population of young workers yet an unemployment problem. The BPO industry addressed this issue and created over one million jobs, decreasing the unemployment rate from 9% in the early 2000s to 4% in 2024.

Increased BPO opportunities also spurred the creation of more businesses in various industries, including real estate, transportation, and food services. With small businesses better economically supported, young professionals have begun to start their careers in diverse fields such as customer service and software development. The IT sector in particular contributed 12.6% of the country's GDP and employed over 1.5 million Filipinos in 2022. That same year, the industry also generated over $40 billion in revenue and became one of the top sources of foreign exchange for the Philippines.[2]

India shares a similar story, although the country gained a reputation for its historic call center industry much earlier than the Philippines. Beginning in the 1980s but skyrocketing in the 1990s, India has a vast and nuanced history with outsourcing. According to a report by the National Association of Software & Services Companies (NASSCOM), nearly half of all Fortune 500 companies choose Indian outsourcing service providers, and 80% of US and European companies rank Indian outsourcing services as their top choice due to their skilled professionals with a strong work ethic.[3] India's GDP is now the fifth-largest in the world, surpassing the UK, France, Brazil, Italy, and Canada.[4] Indian IT outsourcing is projected to generate over $11 billion USD in revenue in 2024 and grow at an annual rate of 13%, resulting in over $20 billion by 2029.[5] It is without doubt that India has earned its title of the biggest outsourcing hub in the world.

Compared to the Philippines and India, talented African tech companies are often overlooked, despite the vast and highly valuable workforce available. These African companies have the knowledge and expertise to provide the same services for international companies at an identical quality and potentially even at a cheaper rate, especially as Asian counterparts become more and more saturated. However, several problems, notably in Ethiopia, continue to discourage foreign investors and outsourcing companies.

First, certain policies currently place limitations on foreign outsourcing companies and investors. For example, when foreign investors provide seed funding to startups, the government charges a "capital gains" tax. By definition, capital gains taxes occur *after* the sale of an asset, not on initial investments. Other unnecessary taxes like these pose significant obstacles to a built-out BPO industry, including excessive import taxes on vital materials for starting and running these businesses. Rather than providing tax incentives to jumpstart this sector and greatly transform the economy, the government instead penalizes incoming foreign companies, discouraging their participation in Ethiopian markets.

Secondly, changing conversion rates further complicate international business, especially when these changes are drastic. In 2023, 500,000 ETB would have been equivalent to about $9,000 USD, but in August 2024, this same amount of ETB equaled about $4,400 USD. This dramatic shift occurred because, on July 29, Ethiopia's central bank floated the birr currency in order to secure a $3.4 billion IMF (International Monetary Fund) package. Three weeks later, the birr lost half of its value and began to trade at 74.73 against the US dollar, whereas it had been trading at 57.48 birr to the dollar.[6]

Although this seems like an unfavorable development, Prime Minister Abiy deems it necessary as part of a long-term strategy to help with inflation and foreign investment. He referred to this reform as "the pain of surgery, endured for healing."[7] While the move does help with import restrictions, importing the same goods now costs double. If Ethiopia wants to maintain the ability to trade internationally, a more stable conversion rate is key.

Cultural differences also pose a considerable challenge to foreign investors and companies. Ethiopia is the only African state never to have been colonized by the West, and while this is a historically celebrated fact due to Ethiopia's preserved history, it also fosters a tradition-centered mindset where people resist change and lack exposure to other cultures. For this reason, few Ethiopians can fluently speak English, French, Italian, or any of the world's more widely spoken business languages.[8] Ethiopia's lack of cultural diffusion even extends to its calendar. Most of the world tracks the passing of time using the Gregorian calendar while Ethiopia uses its own: the Ge'ez calendar. Based upon the ancient Coptic Calendar, the Ethiopian calendar is seven to eight years behind the Gregorian calendar.[9] The difference in dates and times may be confusing to foreign companies and their clients, and it may cause simple but frequent misunderstandings in the workplace for Ethiopians, especially when in conjunction with any language barriers.

Finally, the most noteworthy obstacle, especially in the aftermath of the COVID-19 pandemic and the drastic uptick in remote work, is the very issue Prime Minister Abiy has centered his platform around: digital transformation.

Internet Freedom

In May 2023, the Ethiopian Ministry of Transport and Logistics introduced a digital payment system for fuel retail. In the first two days, over 43,000 transactions were made via the new system—a testament to Prime Minister Abiy's dedication to digital transformation. The payment system was intended to reduce corruption in the fuel retail industry while also alleviating Ethiopia's cash shortage by banning cash transactions at all gas stations in the country.

Addis Ababa, which is home to 60% of the vehicles in the country and consumes 65% of the approximately 12 million liters of fuel the nation uses daily, was only given an 18-day notice before gas stations went cashless. One day, drivers paid with cash, and then the next day, the evening news announced the strict digital payment system with zero cash accepted. This seemingly immediate and cold-turkey switch incited annoyance and confusion. Despite the government claiming the system was tested for months, customers and fuel retailers alike faced slow transaction times, challenges with payment confirmation, and perhaps the biggest barrier: the low digital literacy of most Ethiopians.

In the Western world, credit and debit cards are the most common methods of payment. However, in Ethiopia, cash is the primary option. Most Ethiopians do not own bank cards, let alone see the value in paying directly from their phones, so customers struggled when using the digital system to pay. Many could not remember their usernames and passwords and frustratingly had to use one-time verification passwords to access their accounts. Limited digital literacy, combined with slow internet connections and delays in SMS purchase confirmations, caused extremely long wait times for gas, sometimes taking 20 minutes for a payment to go through. These delays even pushed some customers to fill up their tanks and drive away without paying while gas station employees attempted to work the system.

The abrupt change made customers panic. Thinking the new system would fail, people began lining up at gas stations to purchase large quantities of fuel in preparation. This resulted in even longer lines, increased activity at gas stations, and a detrimental fuel shortage, which impacted the more than 700,000 vehicles registered in Addis Ababa.[10]

This disorienting move to digital payment is only one example of a larger problem: The digital illiteracy of the public paired with the poor digital planning of the government—in addition to internal conflict and inefficiency—creates an unwelcome environment for foreign businesses looking to expand into Ethiopia. A paradox is thereby created. The government wishes to invite more international companies yet limits internet freedom, the one essential component needed for these companies to function in the country.

In 2016, the government temporarily shut down the internet after massive protests in two of the biggest states in the country, losing the economy approximately $123 million USD. This number pales in comparison to Tigray, which went without reliable internet, telecommunications, and banking over the course of two years due to war.[11] In 2022, Tigray, with a population of five million people, had no internet connection for a total of 8,760 hours (365 days), making it the world's longest uninterrupted shutdown.

Such outages result in dire consequences for both public and private businesses. Businesses, which rely on a stable internet connection, could not function, and banks, hospitals, and other critical services were also impaired. With consideration to how this issue raises nuanced questions about free speech, it also presents an urgent concern with outsourcing opportunities. Foreign companies are hesitant to invest in a country or establish BPO businesses where internet access is unreliable. If these businesses established a company in Ethiopia and the government chose to limit internet usage again, these international companies would have to cease operations within the country and lose out on mass amounts of revenue.

In order to *execute* Prime Minister Abiy's digital transformation strategy, which in part means inviting more foreign investment opportunities into the country, Ethiopia will need more secure and dependable networks, in addition to intentional pushes for digital literacy. Even if both of those necessary components are obtained, another primary fear is that the Ethiopian government will monitor international data, which presents a security concern for foreign nations. When international companies enter the Ethiopian market, they want not only internet reliability but also internet freedom—a politically liberated internet that is not influenced or censored by federal entities.

Untapped Potential

In January 2012, the 18th ordinary session of the Assembly of Heads of State and Government of the African Union was held in Addis Ababa, Ethiopia. There, African officials determined the need for a trade agreement that would promote socioeconomic growth and development across the continent—and unite African trade on a holistic level.

The African Continental Free Trade Area (AfCFTA) agreement was signed on March 21, 2019 in Kigali, Rwanda, and put into effect on May 30. The AfCFTA aims to merge 55 economies into a single, competitive mega market of more than a billion people, making it one of the biggest free trade areas in the world.[12] This agreement will make it easier for Africa to trade with other continents as well as among African countries. It has immense potential to reduce poverty and broaden economic inclusion, along with several other objectives:

- Create a single African market for goods and services, which will remove trade barriers, ease the movement of goods, and streamline the way businesses, especially small businesses, trade

- Reduce taxes, tariffs, and customs delays[13]
- Lift 30 million Africans out of extreme poverty and boost the incomes of nearly 68 million others who live on less than $5.50 a day
- Boost Africa's income by $450 billion by 2035 while adding $76 billion to the income of the rest of the world
- Increase Africa's exports by $560 billion[14]

Ethiopia ratified the AfCFTA agreement in March 2019, partially in its effort to open up the economy and adhere to Prime Minister Abiy's plan to invite foreign involvement. The country's participation in AfCFTA directly references its willingness to welcome BPO companies as well. The more open Ethiopia is in all areas, trade included, the more likely international investors and companies will view it as a prime location for business.

Currently, Ethiopia is a "sleeping giant" in outsourcing. Unlocking such massive untapped potential would revolutionize daily life, be a rare strategic advantage for foreign companies, and make a lasting impact on Africa as a whole.

The benefits for international companies are numerous:
- Ethiopia is the second-most populous country in Africa with over 70% of the population under the age of 30.
- Land, labor, and energy costs are low in comparison to other African markets.
- Ethiopia has a very low attrition rate compared to other outsourcing destinations.
- Very little competition exists in Ethiopian markets, allowing foreign companies to be the first to seize this opportunity and establish their brands before others.

Likewise, the benefits to Ethiopia cannot be overstated:

- An increase in BPOs would drastically and quickly lower the unemployment rate, therefore enhancing the quality of life for citizens.

- The issue of Ethiopia's high import costs would be solved. The economy has been undermined for decades because Ethiopia's import costs far outweigh export revenue. Despite exporting more than $4 billion worth of goods in 2022, Ethiopia still spent $12 billion on imports, leaving the country in a deficit of $8 billion.[15] The introduction of a solidified BPO industry could solve this problem as there will be a significant opportunity for increased foreign currency.

- Like in the Philippines, the private business sector would be better supported and lead to an increase in small businesses across diverse industries, such as real estate and technology.

At IE Networks, we are working to enjoy these benefits while also improving the work we offer clients. While most companies develop software to sell to other companies, we have been developing software solutions to automate our internal operations, implementing tools to help with supply chain management, HR, and transportation. Because of this, our team is able to fix bugs, add upgrades, and implement new services to the software quickly and based on our changing needs. These services also come with data-driven AI capabilities to make all processes move faster and more efficiently.

In the future, our goal is to outsource this software development service to other companies in Europe and the US, commercialized as SaaS. More than just software development, we would like to outsource other services like network, data center, or infrastructure services so that employees can complete network design, server implementation, or other related work for companies that need the extra support at a cheaper rate. IE Networks has the talent, the knowledge, and the people who are ready to work. Outsourcing would help revolutionize what the company is capable of while continuing to positively affect Ethiopia, making it the next cutting-edge hub for outsourcing.

With the advantages of foreign involvement clear to businesses like ours, citizens, and government officials, federal change is on the horizon. In April 2024, the Ethiopian Investment Board "guardedly" enacted a law permitting foreign participation in the import, export, wholesale, and retail trade businesses.[16] Additionally, several global companies have expressed interest in investing in Ethiopia, especially as new legislation and policies continue to emerge and boost the benefits of doing so. Ethiopian Ambassador to Pakistan Jemal Beker said one of Ethiopia's main tenets of foreign policy is to attract Foreign Direct Investment (FDI) and foreign companies.[17] Some companies have already been granted licenses to invest in horticulture and pharmaceuticals while companies in other industries, notably manufacturing and agriculture, are requesting to invest.

It is ultimately the government's responsibility to create an attractive and enabling environment for international companies so that Ethiopia can begin competing on a global scale. However, citizens can also play a role in facilitating change. More people from private-sector backgrounds should have a voice and position in the government. That experience should be used to make informed changes that will support the development of businesses. More organizations and associations should also be created and empowered to lend insight to government officials from a perspective of private business, making space for politicians to hear what businesses *need* to continue thriving.

In April 2024, Ethiopia launched the Digital Transformation Council led by the deputy prime minister, which "amalgamates influential figures from both the public and private sectors, setting the stage for an unprecedented push toward a digital economy."[18] Unfortunately, while this may *seem* like a productive forum in which both public and private sectors can meet to make technology-forward decisions—in reality, it is operating as a government authority. The council only strengthens the government's controlling position in the private sector, and there needs to be a meaningful pivot. With increased thoughts from experienced entrepreneurs and business leaders, ideas can cease being just that—ideas—and instead become realities.

Many Ethiopians may be resistant to this change I'm proposing: one of a truly free and open market, rife with competition and shifts from tradition. But the main outcome here transcends profit, GDP, and finances. It is more than increased trade and more than investment opportunities to line foreign pockets. The main outcome is that in the next 10–30 years, the most productive world population will be in African countries, and an influx of jobs will stabilize the economy. Young people will have reliable incomes and consistent work. They will be able to care for their families, afford necessities like food and healthcare, and begin exploring their interests and lives, not simply surviving or "getting by." A more open country will enable people to vacation and experience the world without concern that they may never return to their home country—better yet, they will be able to move countries without putting Ethiopia's economy at risk. In other words, young people will have something to protect, something to look forward to, something to build and make their own.

And when these young people have good-paying jobs and lives they love, they won't want war or conflict—they will demand peace and compromise. What is more important than building the foundation for that?

ETHIOPIA
INCORPORATED

A book can do more than portray a message. It can inspire others toward action. It can leave behind a permanent footprint for the author. It can change lives, potentially even a nation. Perhaps even the world.

I have read many biographies and memoirs about the most successful entrepreneurs in history: Steve Jobs, Warren Buffet, Bill Gates, Elon Musk. I have also read the stories of historical figures like Benjamin Franklin and Thomas Jefferson, taking in the good and bad, how they made an impact, and how they reached the precipice of their lives, which would eventually influence society on a global level. Even reading the biography of John D. Rockefeller, one of the wealthiest Americans of all time, I recognized his arrogance and greed, but beyond that, I understood a hidden story of entrepreneurship, one where someone builds an empire from nothing. These books allow you to see through popular opinion and what you may already know, instead letting you view a nuanced, complex individual for who they truly were and what they believed. Rather than a simple historical document, these books tap into the heart of the "why," the secrets to inspiration, and the reasoning behind how great people are pushed to do even greater things.

Much like these popular figures, I have always envisioned writing a book—I simply thought I would do so in retirement, not at the peak of my career. I imagined stepping back from IE Networks, teaching at a university, and putting together a *textbook* for my classes, never a business memoir. That expectation for my future was drastically reworked and expedited, however, when more and more young people began approaching me, online and in person. Whenever a new podcast, article, or interview comes out featuring my brand or IE Networks, I am stopped in airports and restaurants so that these young people can shake my hand. At tech conferences and local entrepreneurial events, new workers look to me with hungry eyes, eager to soak up whatever knowledge I can give them within a brief interaction. I even receive countless LinkedIn messages asking for advice. Each time, I think about how a short conversation is not enough and how I wish I could sit each person down to talk in-depth about their ideas and, most importantly, the execution of them. If I had an entrepreneurial mentor who did that for me back when starting IE Networks, many challenges would have been solved quicker and with much less frustration.

My hope is that this book can be that mentor in this country of many complexities. Ethiopia struggles with deeply ingrained political, cultural, and economic challenges: past ties to communism, educational deficiencies, financial corruption, and more. As a solution, the country focuses on small issues, such as digital payment systems and requiring more taxes, rather than the big picture: how to take itself out of poverty. This is demoralizing for people who have great aspirations but nowhere to channel them. When the economy does not feed such ambition, the emboldened thinkers of our time try to push ahead, work harder than the people around them, and eventually burn out, seeing that their hard work just puts them in the same place as the rest of their peers. Anyone would give up after hitting a brick wall enough times, even those with the potential for greatness.

This book is not a destructive critique of Ethiopia or its people; it is a problem-solution guide to identifying areas for improvement. I love my country and what I have been able to build here. Therefore, this book does not aim to paint Ethiopia, or Africa as a whole, in a negative light or assert that the country's challenges are insurmountable. Rather, it is a pathway forward for change-makers, one that says, "I see what you are going through because I have been there myself. Here's what needs to change, and here's how we, collectively, change it." Again, it is a mentor for young graduates, entrepreneurs, government officials, and potential foreign investors—all the people who will carve out legacies for themselves as they make an unprecedented impact.

Instead of having a business idea but thinking it impossible, I want people to remain energized, pursue their passions, and see that even someone from humble beginnings can make a name for themselves. These challenges with finance, manpower, and bureaucracy will never be solved unless *we* solve them. Lamenting the current state of things behind closed doors has never, historically, made a difference. But when you speak out in the right place at the right time to the right people, then a solution is officially put out into the world and considered. Better yet, when you speak out and take *action* toward the solution independently, you directly contribute. You *become* the solution.

You may have been born in an impoverished part of the world without certain privileges, where it is easy to feel like you lost the "geographical lottery" and fate has predetermined your future, no matter what steps you take to change it. However, no matter your circumstances or challenges, your life is built on your choices, and even the smallest actions toward progress can add up to make a significant impact. Who you should compete with is not another person, your government, or even fate—but your prior self from yesterday.

In a country where many feel powerless in the face of very serious, very debilitating issues, such as hunger, poor healthcare systems, and war, sometimes the most daring action is to better your own life. Continuous improvement is contagious. A simple shift in attitude or perspective can influence your neighbor to do the same. From there, they could influence the people around them, spreading beyond anyone's imagination in a way that may not be readily apparent but does affect the very core of the nation. If we can do this—break the cycle of complacency to succeed within difficult landscapes—we will be making it even easier for our children to succeed as well. No matter your profession—accountant, lawyer, politician, teacher—a change in mindset can change your direction. And that collective impact will change the world in ways you may never *see* but ways that do exist and do matter. It is never too late to begin improving your life, thereby improving the lives of others around you.

I had never touched a computer until my second year of college. Before, I was a studious learner who bounced between potential occupations. Maybe I could have been a pilot, a doctor, or an economist. At one point, I even considered studying theology. I came from a poor family with limited opportunities, but I knew that if I studied hard and chose the correct path, I could find a way to improve our lives. Despite all my potential career choices, I never once considered entrepreneurship. I didn't know of anyone who had pursued it, and no one ever discussed it as a viable option.

I find it difficult to reconcile with this, now understanding that the *only* way forward is through business. An open market. Free trade. More financial freedom and investment opportunities for entrepreneurs. Tax incentives. Government support. International involvement and competition, particularly in the form of outsourcing. Every problem can be helped by entrepreneurs. In fact, they *must* be part of *every* solution as business is the sustainable foundation for all industries: healthcare, agriculture, education, finance, banking, construction, manufacturing, technology, retail, real estate, and every other imaginable sector. Where there are challenges, there is also opportunity. And entrepreneurship is the pathway to that opportunity, no matter your background, country, or passion.

Working from such a broad national viewpoint, it is easy to say much federal work must be done before any true improvements are made. But if people believe that they can change, it is possible to change. If Ethiopia is to flourish with a robust private sector, it must run like a company itself—a company called Ethiopia Incorporated, a unification of many arms that come together to identify problems, brainstorm innovative solutions, accept investments, and generate revenue. A company with clear and transparent hierarchies, OKRs, communicated expectations and consequences, and a value proposition that signifies a greater objective—one that people can truly rally around.

Most importantly, Ethiopia Incorporated must have a mission statement understood by everyone in the company, from the new hires to the executives: *Transform African businesses, and transform life as a result.*

While I hope that *Ethiopia Incorporated* motivates you to start your entrepreneurial journey, no book can cover everything you need to know for launching a business, especially in complex environments such as Ethiopia.

Visit www.ethiopia-incorporated.com to discover more entrepreneurial resources, learn more about IE Networks's mission, and access a global network of business professionals. I also encourage you to email share@ethiopia-incorporated.com and share your journey so far. Thank you for reading.

I look forward to hearing from you and wish you the best of luck.

ACKNOWLEDGMENTS

I have to start by thanking my mother, Emebet Zewdie, who made sure I got everything for my education from my early childhood until I graduated from Mekelle University and who later became a guarantor for my CCIE expenses.

I would like to thank Menberu Bekele (my dear brother), Dr. Abiyot Bayou, Dr. Ahmedin Mohammed, Dr. Yohannes Alemseged, Dr. Zelalem Assefa, Amare Herpie, Anteneh Awoke, Biniam G. Hiwet, Debbol Shenkute, Robel Kitaba, Tibebeselassie A. Tedla, Tigabu Haile, Tsigabu Welu, Tihitna Mulushewa Legess, and Zelalem Chalachew for reviewing the manuscript and providing valuable feedback.

To the team at BrightRay, especially Jamie Fleming, thank you for supporting me in making my distant dream of writing a book happen so early.

To my long-time friends and industry family, of whom there are too many to list, thank you all. From early on in my career to starting my own business, there were so many of you who guided me, supported me, and celebrated the milestones with me. Thank you for being my sounding board, my confidants, and my friends.

NOTES

Introduction

1. This saying is attributed to the Roman philosopher Seneca.

Chapter One

1. "Haile Gebrselassie," Olympics, accessed September 24, 2024, https://olympics.com/en/athletes/haile-gebrselassie.

2. "Ethiopia's Olympic Hero Embarks on 11th Hotel Investment," New Business, February 7, 2022, https://newbusinessethiopia.com/investment/ethiopias-olympic-hero-embarks-on-11th-hotel-investment/.

3. "Haile Gebrselassie," New York Road Runners, accessed September 24, 2024, https://www.nyrr.org/about/hall-of-fame/haile-gebrselassie.

4. "Haile Gebrselassie," Olympedia, accessed September 24, 2024, https://www.olympedia.org/athletes/67405.

5. Rahel Samuel, "New-African Magazine Announces the 100 Most Influential Africans of 2013," Ethiosports, December 1, 2013, https://www.ethiosports.com/2013/12/01/new-african-magazine-announces-the-100-most-influential-africans-of-2013/.

6. John Sparks, "Olympic Legend and Now Successful Businessman Haile Gebrselassie Warns West Not to Push Ethiopia," Sky News, July 8, 2021, https://news.sky.com/story/olympic-legend-turned-successful-businessman-haile-gebrselassie-warns-west-not-to-push-ethiopia-12351681.

7. Jim Denison, *The Greatest: The Haile Gebrselassie Story* (Breakaway Books, 2011).

8. "IOM Alarmed by Deaths of 27 Ethiopian Migrants in Zambia," International Organization for Migration, December 12, 2022, https://www.iom.int/news/iom-alarmed-deaths-27-ethiopian-migrants-zambia.

Chapter Two

1. "The Kingdom of Aksum," National Geographic, updated October 19, 2023, https://education.nationalgeographic.org/resource/kingdom-aksum/.

2. "Italo-Ethiopian War," Britannica, updated September 10, 2024, https://www.britannica.com/event/Italo-Ethiopian-War-1935-1936.

3. Thomas P. Ofcansky and LaVerle Berry, *Ethiopia: A Country Study* (Library of Congress, 1991).

4. "Developments of the 1950s and 1960s," Together We Learn, accessed September 24, 2024, https://twlethiopia.org/article/19-developments-of-the-1950s-and-1960s/.

5. "Ethiopia Profile - Timeline," BBC, October 12, 2020, https://www.bbc.com/news/world-africa-13351397.

6. "Socialist Ethiopia (1974–91)," Britannica, updated August 20, 2024, https://www.britannica.com/place/Ethiopia/Socialist-Ethiopia-1974-91.

7. "Prime Minister Abiy Ahmed's Inaugural Address to the Ethiopian Parliament in Addis Ababa," *International Journal of Ethiopian Studies* 12, no. 2 (April 2018): 193–98, https://www.jstor.org/stable/27026562?read-now=1&seq=2.

8. "The World Bank in Ethiopia," World Bank Group, updated April 9, 2024, https://www.worldbank.org/en/country/ethiopia/overview.

9. "Ethiopia Population (Live)," Worldometer, accessed September 24, 2024, https://www.worldometers.info/world-population/ethiopia-population/.

10. "Learning and Development!," UNICEF Ethiopia, accessed September 24, 2024, https://www.unicef.org/ethiopia/learning-and-development.

11. "Study in Ethiopia," Free Apply, accessed September 24, 2024, https://free-apply.com/en/articles/country/337996.

12. "Education and Youth," USAID, accessed September 24, 2024, https://www.usaid.gov/ethiopia/education.

13. "What We Do," UNICEF Ethiopia, accessed September 24, 2024, https://www.unicef.org/ethiopia/what-we-do.

14. "Healthcare," Ethiopia - Country Commercial Guide, International Trade Administration, January 18, 2024, https://www.trade.gov/country-commercial-guides/ethiopia-healthcare.

15. Janet Moore, "Ethiopian Entrepreneurs: Five Inspiring Women and Men to Watch," Distant Horizons, May 27, 2020, https://www.distant-horizons.com/ethiopia-a-new-hot-spot-for-ethiopian-entrepreneurs-distant-horizons/.

16. "The World's Finest Handmade Runner," soleRebels, accessed September 24, 2024, https://www.solerebels.com/.

17. "Ethiopia Construction Market Size, Trend Analysis by Sector, Competitive Landscape and Forecast to 2028," GlobalData, updated June 19, 2024, https://www.globaldata.com/store/report/ethiopia-construction-market-analysis.

18. Charles Matseke, "Ethiopa-China Relations," Centre for Africa-China Studies, accessed September 24, 2024, https://www.cacs.org.za/ethiopia-china-relations/.

19. "Chinese Companies Taking Over Ethiopia's Construction Industry," Ethiopian Business Review, June 2023, https://ethiopianbusinessreview.net/chinese-companies-taking-over-ethiopias-construction-industry-2/.

20. "Agriculture and Food Security," USAID, accessed September 24, 2024, https://www.usaid.gov/ethiopia/agriculture-and-food-security.

21. "Timeline: Ethiopia," Oxford Reference, accessed September 24, 2024, https://www.oxfordreference.com/display/10.1093/acref/9780191735783.timeline.0001.

22. *Coffee Annual* (United States Department of Agriculture Report ET2022-0018, 2022), https://apps.fas.usda.gov/newgainapi/api/Report/DownloadReportByFileName?fileName=Coffee%20Annual_Addis%20Ababa_Ethiopia_ET2022-0018.pdf.

23. Chinedu Okafor, "Ethiopia's Coffee Exports Soar, Generates $1.43 Billion in Revenue," Business Insider Africa, July 11, 2024, https://africa.businessinsider.

com/local/markets/ethiopias-coffee-exports-hit-dollar143-billion-in-202324/0fmk33g.

24. Mengesha Amare, "Ethiopia: Efforts to Boost Agricultural Mechanization," AllAfrica, June 6, 2024, https://allafrica.com/stories/202406060302.html.

25. "About Ethiopia," Embassy of Ethiopia, accessed September 24, 2024, https://ethiopianembassy.org/overview-about-ethiopia/.

26. "Matthew 19:24," YouVersion, accessed September 24, 2024, https://www.bible.com/bible/1/MAT.19.24. KJV.

Chapter Three

1. "Market Overview," Ethiopia - Country Commercial Guide, International Trade Administration, January 18, 2024, https://www.trade.gov/country-commercial-guides/ethiopia-market-overview.

2. "Agro-Processing," Ethiopia - Country Commercial Guide, International Trade Administration, January 18, 2024, https://www.trade.gov/country-commercial-guides/ethiopia-agro-processing.

3. "Agricultural Sectors," Ethiopia - Country Commercial Guide, International Trade Administration, January 18, 2024, https://www.trade.gov/country-commercial-guides/ethiopia-agricultural-sectors.

4. "Scaling Up Climate Ambition on Land Use and Agriculture through Nationally Determined Contributions and National Adaptation Plans (SCALA)," Food and Agriculture Organization of the United Nations, accessed September 24, 2024, https://www.fao.org/in-action/scala/countries/ethiopia/en.

5. "Market Overview," Ethiopia - Country Commercial Guide, International Trade Administration, January 18, 2024, https://www.trade.gov/country-commercial-guides/ethiopia-market-overview.

6. "Communist Dictatorship in Ethiopia (1974–1991)," Communist Crimes, Estonian Institute of Historical Memory, accessed September 24, 2024, https://communistcrimes.org/en/countries/ethiopia.

7. Arch Puddington, "Ethiopia: The Communist Uses of Famine," Commentary, April 1986, https://www.commentary.org/articles/arch-puddington-2/ethiopia-the-communist-uses-of-famine/.

8. "2020 Investment Climate Statements: Ethiopia," US Department of State, accessed September 24, 2024, https://www.state.gov/reports/2020-investment-climate-statements/ethiopia/.

9. "About Us," Ethiopian Investment Holdings, accessed September 24, 2024, https://eih.et/about-us.

10. "Ethiopian Investment Holdings," IFSWF, accessed September 24, 2024, https://www.ifswf.org/members/ethiopian-investment-holdings.

11. "About," Ethiopian Airlines, accessed September 24, 2024, https://corporate.ethiopianairlines.com/AboutEthiopian/Overview.

12. Gioia Shah, "Ethiopian Airlines Boss Calls for African Aviation Deregulation to Lower Costs for Travellers," Financial Times, August 20, 2024, https://www.ft.com/content/b986faf2-7398-4df2-a5bd-f7a3c140f448.

13. Annual Report 2022/2023 (National Bank of Ethiopia, 2024), https://nbe.gov.et/wp-content/uploads/2024/08/Annual-Report-2022-2023.pdf.

13. "How Many Banks Are There in Ethiopia," Talking Ethiopia, July 8, 2024, https://talkingethiopia.com/how-many-banks-are-there-in-ethiopia/.

14. *Quarterly Macroeconomic Updates on the Ethiopian Economy* 9, no. 2 (August 2024): https://doi.org/10.13140/RG.2.2.21907.08487.

15. "Ethiopia Banking Sector Opportunities," International Trade Administration, accessed September 24, 2024, https://www.trade.gov/market-intelligence/ethiopia-banking-sector-opportunities.

16. Duncan Miriri, "Ethiopia Opens Up to Foreign Investment Firms Ahead of Capital Markets Launch," Reuters, January 18, 2024, https://www.reuters.com/markets/ethiopia-opens-up-foreign-investment-firms-ahead-capital-markets-launch-2024-01-18/.

17. "Overview of ESL," Ethiopian Shipping & Logistics, accessed September 24, 2024, https://www.eslse.et/overview.php.

18. Tom Gardner, "Ethiopia Opens Up Budding Logistics Sector," The Africa Report, March 20, 2019, https://www.theafricareport.com/10463/ethiopia-opens-up-budding-logistics-sector/.

19. "Ministry Ends Age-Old Logistics Monopoly, Partially," Addis Fortune, October 9, 2021, https://addisfortune.news/ministry-ends-age-old-logistics-monopoly-partially/.

20. "Ethiopian Shipping Lines Monopoly Proves Harder to Break than Hoped," Africa Intelligence, March 22, 2024, https://www.africaintelligence.com/eastern-africa-and-the-horn/2024/03/22/ethiopian-shipping-lines-monopoly-proves-harder-to-break-than-hoped,110194977-art.

21. "Brief Historical Review of Telecom Sector in Ethiopia," Ethio Telecom, accessed September 24, 2024, https://www.ethiotelecom.et/history/#.

22. Alexander Winning and Tim Cocks, "Combatants in Ethiopia's Tigray War Agree to Stop Fighting," Reuters, November 2, 2022, https://www.reuters.com/world/africa/african-union-parties-ethiopia-conflict-have-agreed-cease-hostilities-2022-11-02/.

23. Paula Gilbert, "Bigger Stake in Ethio Telecom Now Up for Grabs," Connecting Africa, February 10, 2023, https://www.connectingafrica.com/author.asp?section_id=761&doc_id=783178.

24. "Joint Ventures in India," Lexology, October 27, 2021, https://www.lexology.com/library/detail.aspx?g=2baad873-02c7-41b6-a585-a1121954144b.

25. "UAE Moves Toward 100% Foreign Ownership of Companies," Hegazy and Partners, accessed September 24, 2024, https://www.hegazylaw.com/uae-moves-toward-100-foreign-ownership-of-companies/.

26. "The 60-40 Equity Rule on Owning a Business in the Philippines," Duran & Duran-Schulze Law, accessed September 24, 2024, https://duranschulze.com/the-60-40-equity-rule-on-owning-a-business-in-the-philippines/.

27. Bukola Adebayo, "Ethiopia Opens Airline and Telecoms to Private, International Investors," WKBT News 8 Now, June 6, 2018, https://www.news8000.com/lifestyle/ethiopia-opens-airline-and-telecoms-to-private-international-investors/article_cdc966dd-ad8c-55a3-8201-9458eaaf394f.html.

28. Kaleyesus Bekele, "Now Ethiopian Has a Private Eye," Times Aerospace, March 21, 2024, https://www. timesaerospace.aero/features/general-aviation/now-ethiopian-has-a-private-eye.

Chapter Four

1. "Samrawit Fikru," Ethiopian Business Review, April 15, 2019, https://ethiopianbusinessreview.net/samrawit-fikru/.

2. Oluwafisayo Dorcas Adeyooye, "Meet Samrawit Fikru, the Tech Genius Reforming Ethiopia's Transport Sector," Built In Africa, accessed September 24, 2024, https://www.builtinafrica.io/videos/samrawit-fikru.

3. Miklol Girma, "The Evolution of Ride-Hailing Services in Ethiopia," Reqiq Insights, June 4, 2024, https:// reqiq.co/the-evolution-of-ride-hailing-services-in-ethiopia/.

4. Birhanu Fikade, "Authority to Ban Uber-Styled Transport Service," The Reporter, November 3, 2018, https://www.thereporterethiopia.com/6732/.

5. "City Officials Renew Drive to Breathe Down on Ride-Hailing Companies," Addis Fortune, July 2, 2022, https://addisfortune.news/city-officials-renew-drive-to-breathe-down-on-ride-hailing-companies/.

6. "Samrawit Fikru," Rest of World, accessed September 24, 2024, https://restofworld.org/profile/samrawit-fikru/.

7. "Growth and Transformation Plan II," United Nations Ethiopia, August 28, 2019, https://ethiopia.un.org/ en/15231-growth-and-transformation-plan-ii.

8. "Starting a Business," Doing Business, accessed September 24, 2024, https://archive.doingbusiness.org/en/data/exploretopics/starting-a-business.

9. Belete Molla Getahun, "The Challenges and Opportunities with Ethiopia's Digital Transformation," World Economic Forum, March 18, 2024, https://www.weforum.org/agenda/2024/03/bridging-the-digital-divide-challenges-and-opportunities-for-ethiopias-digital-transformation/.

Chapter Five

1. Now, when obtaining a personal loan from a friend or family member, the recommended course of action is to visit a government office together and sign an official personal loan agreement. You will be required to pay a 2% service tax to the government, a far cry from the 30% required in the event of an audit.

2. Johanna Söderström and Camille Pellerin, "Tax Evasion is Rife in Ethiopia Despite the Government Crackdown," *The London School of Economics and Political Science* (blog), July 11, 2023, https://blogs.lse.ac.uk/africaatlse/2023/07/11/tax-evasion-is-rife-in-ethiopia-despite-the-government-crackdown/.

3. Esmael Abdu and Mohammd Adem, "Tax Compliance Behavior of Taxpayers in Ethiopia: A Review Paper," *Cogent Economics & Finance* 11, no. 1 (March 2023): https://doi.org/10.1080/23322039.2023.2189559.

4. Johanna Söderström and Camille Pellerin, "Tax Evasion is Rife in Ethiopia Despite the Government Crackdown," *The London School of Economics and Political Science* (blog), July 11, 2023, https://blogs.lse.ac.uk/africaatlse/2023/07/11/tax-evasion-is-rife-in-ethiopia-despite-the-government-crackdown/.

5. Leon Schreiber, "Funding Development: Ethiopia Tries to Strengthen Its Tax System, 2007–2018 (Short Version)," *Innovations for Successful Societies* (Trustees of Princeton University, 2018), https://successfulsocieties.princeton.edu/sites/g/files/toruqf5601/files/TD_Ethiopia_Revenue_Short_Formatted_5.2.19%20electronic.pdf.

6. Dasalegn Mosissa Jalata, "The Value Added Tax and Sales Tax in Ethiopia: A Comparative Overview," *European Journal of Business and Management* 6, no. 23 (2014) https://citeseerx.ist.psu.edu/document?repid=rep1&type=pdf&doi=092c608d2d8112798d8275af746c5e61d20a25bc.

7. "Corporate - Withholding Taxes," PWC, August 14, 2024, https://taxsummaries.pwc.com/ethiopia/corporate/withholding-taxes.

8. *The Government of Ethiopia Unveiled a Major Revision of Tariffs on Imported Goods* (United States Department of Agriculture Report ET2021-0002, 2021), https://apps.fas.usda.gov/newgainapi/api/Report/DownloadReportByFileName?fileName=The%20Government%20of%20Ethiopia%20Unveiled%20a%20Major%20Revision%20of%20Tariffs%20on%20Imported%20Goods_Addis%20Ababa_Ethiopia_08-06-2021.pdf.

9. "Gov't Introduces Social Welfare Tax as Budget Deficit Widens," Addis Fortune, August 13, 2022, https://addisfortune.news/govt-introduces-social-welfare-tax-as-budget-deficit-widens/.

10. "2023 Investment Climate Statements: Kenya," US Department of State, accessed September 24, 2024,

https://www.state.gov/reports/2023-investment-climate-statements/kenya/.

11. "Doing Business in Kenya: Overview," Thomas Reuters Practical Law, March 1, 2022, https://content.next.westlaw.com/practical-law/document/I5b4d222e13bc11e798dc8b09b4f043e0/Doing-Business-in-Kenya-Overview?viewType=FullText&transitionType=Default&contextData=(sc.Default).

12. Tom Harris and Edris Seid, *2019/20 Survey of the Ethiopian Tax System* (Institute for Fiscal Studies Report R187, 2021), https://www.taxdev.org/sites/default/files/2021-04/R187-2019-20-Survey-of-the-Ethiopian-tax-system.pdf.

Chapter Six

1. Yinebeb Bahru, "Digital Lending Platforms," *United Nations Development Programme Ethiopia* (blog), January 30, 2024, https://www.undp.org/ethiopia/blog/digital-lending-platforms.

2. Tewedaj Sintayehu, "Options to Finance SMEs," *The Reporter*, July 10, 2021, https://www.thereporterethiopia.com/11658/.

3. Nathnael Tsegaw and Michael Tomas, *Founder's Guide to Fundraising: Ethiopia*, ed. David Saunders, Lisa With, and Sam Ajadi (Deutsche Gesellschaft für Internationale Zusammenarbeit, 2023), https://static1.squarespace.com/static/5ab2a4d655b02c29746fc58c/t/6368b958a1ec3303b15293b5/1667807609481/Founder%27s+Guide+to+Fundraising+in+Ethiopia.pdf.

4. *Fourth Quarter 2022/23* (National Bank of Ethiopia Quarterly Bulletin, 2023), https://nbe.gov.et/wp-content/uploads/2023/12/Fourth-Quarter-Report-2022-23.pdf.

5. Yinebeb Bahru, "Digital Lending Platforms," *United Nations Development Programme Ethiopia* (blog), January 30, 2024, https://www.undp.org/ethiopia/blog/digital-lending-platforms.

6. Nathnael Tsegaw and Michael Tomas, *Founder's Guide to Fundraising: Ethiopia*, ed. David Saunders, Lisa With, and Sam Ajadi (Deutsche Gesellschaft für Internationale Zusammenarbeit, 2023), https://static1.squarespace.com/static/5ab2a4d655b02c29746fc58c/t/6368 b958a1ec3303b15293b5/1667807609481/Founder%27s+Guide+to+Fundraising+in+Ethiopia.pdf.

7. "Ethio Telecom Launches Telebirr Digital Financial Services in Partnership with Dashen Bank SC," Ethio Telecom, August 5, 2022, https://www.ethiotelecom.et/ethio-telecom-launches-telebirr-digital-financial-services/4/.

8. Yinebeb Bahru, "Digital Lending Platforms," *United Nations Development Programme Ethiopia* (blog), January 30, 2024, https://www.undp.org/ethiopia/blog/digital-lending-platforms.

9. *A Short Guide to Access DBE's Loans* (Development Bank of Ethiopia), accessed September 24, 2024, https://www.dbe.com.et/BusnessPromotion/Policy/DBENewPolicyEng.pdf.

10. *A Short Guide to Access DBE's Loans* (Development Bank of Ethiopia), accessed September 24, 2024, https://www.dbe.com.et/BusnessPromotion/Policy/DBENewPolicyEng.pdf.

11. "Ethiopia's First Carrier Neutral Data Center," Wingu, accessed September 24, 2024, https://www.wingu.africa/our-locations/addis-ababa-ethiopia/.

12. "Ethiopia's First State-of-the-Art Carrier-Neutral Data Centre," Raxio, accessed September 24, 2024, https://www.raxiogroup.com/locations/ethiopia/.

13. Nathnael Tsegaw and Michael Tomas, *Founder's Guide to Fundraising: Ethiopia*, ed. David Saunders, Lisa With, and Sam Ajadi (Deutsche Gesellschaft für Internationale Zusammenarbeit, 2023), https://static1.squarespace.com/static/5ab2a4d655b02c29746fc58c/t/6368b958a1ec3303b15293b5/1667807609481/Founder%27s+Guide+to+Fundraising+in+Ethiopia.pdf.

14. "2021 Investment Climate Statements: Ethiopia," US Department of State, accessed September 24, 2024, https://www.state.gov/reports/2021-investment-climate-statements/ethiopia/.

15. "Ethiopia Opens Up to Foreign Investment Firms Ahead of Capital Markets Launch," Reuters, January 18, 2024, https://www.reuters.com/markets/ethiopia-opens-up-foreign-investment-firms-ahead-capital-markets-launch-2024-01-18/.

16. "Desire of Foreign Companies to Invest in Ethiopia Growing: Ethiopian Ambassadors," Ethiopian News Agency, January 28, 2024, https://www.ena.et/web/eng/w/eng_3932920.

17. "Home," Ethiopian Securities Exchange, accessed October 14, 2024, https://esxethiopia.com/.

18. "Ethiopian Securities Exchange Garners Over 1.5 Billion Birr, Exceeding Capital-Raising Target," Ethiopian News Agency, April 4, 2024, https://www. ena.et/web/eng/w/eng_4256286#:~:text=As%20 Ethiopia's%20first%20securities%20 exchange,transparency%20and%20corporate%20 governance%20standards.

19. "Progress Towards Ethiopia's Stock Exchange," FSD Africa, accessed September 24, 2024, https:// fsdafrica.org/news/progress-towards-ethiopias-stock-exchange/.

20. "Draft Rulebook of the Ethiopian Securities Exchange," Ethiopian Securities Exchange, accessed September 24, 2024, https://esxethiopia.com/ static/images/rule/file-2024-04-05T07-39-22.112Z-317031898ESXRulebookDraftApril52024.pdf.

21. Lennox Yieke, "Ethiopia Readies Its First Full Stock Market for Launch," African Business, April 3, 2024, https://african.business/2024/04/finance-services/ ethiopia-readies-its-first-full-stock-market-for-launch.

22. "World Bank Supports Ethiopia's Digital ID Project to Increase Access to Services and Economic Opportunities," World Bank Group, December 13, 2023, https://www.worldbank.org/en/news/ press-release/2023/12/13/world-bank-supports-afe-ethiopias-digital-id-project-to-increase-access-to-services-and-economic-opportunities.

23. *Ethiopia: Availability of Fraudulent Identity Documents; State Efforts to Combat Document Fraud (2014–January 2016)* (Immigration and Refugee Board of Canada, 2016), https://webarchive.archive. unhcr.org/20230521134926/https://www.refworld. org/docid/589444d84.html.

24. "NID History," National ID, accessed September 24, 2024, https://id.gov.et/about.

25. Nathnael Tsegaw and Michael Tomas, *Founder's Guide to Fundraising: Ethiopia*, ed. David Saunders, Lisa With, and Sam Ajadi (Deutsche Gesellschaft für Internationale Zusammenarbeit, 2023), https://static1.squarespace.com/static/5ab2a4d655b02c29746fc58c/t/6368b958a1ec3303b15293b5/1667807609481/Founder%27s+Guide+to+Fundraising+in+Ethiopia.pdf.

Chapter Seven

1. *Engineering and Economic Growth: A Global Review* (Cebr for the Royal Academy of Engineering, 2016), https://raeng.org.uk/media/mp2odj00/final-cebr-report-12-09.pdf.

2. Mulu Kahsay, "Quality and Quality Assurance in Ethiopian Higher Education: Critical Issues and Practical Implications," *Journal of Medical Internet Research* (January 2012): https://www.researchgate.net/publication/254860497_Quality_and_quality_assurance_in_Ethiopian_higher_education_critical_issues_and_practical_implications.

3. George West, "Ethiopia's Higher-Education Boom Built on Shoddy Foundations," *The Guardian*, June 22, 2015, https://www.theguardian.com/global-development-professionals-network/2015/jun/22/ethiopia-higher-eduction-universities-development.

4. Zelalem Zekarias Oliso, "Ethiopian Higher Education Expansion and Persisting Challenges: A Systematic Review," *International Journal of Educational Review* 5, no. 1 (March 2023): 11–20, https://ejournal.unib.ac.id/IJER/article/download/26544/11933.

5. "How Many Universities Are There in Ethiopia?," Talking Ethiopia, July 8, 2024, https://talkingethiopia. com/how-many-universities-are-there-in-ethiopia/.

6. Zelalem Zekarias Oliso, "Ethiopian Higher Education Expansion and Persisting Challenges: A Systematic Review," *International Journal of Educational Review* 5, no. 1 (March 2023): 11–20, https://ejournal.unib. ac.id/IJER/article/download/26544/11933.

7. George West, "Ethiopia's Higher-Education Boom Built on Shoddy Foundations," *The Guardian*, June 22, 2015, https://www.theguardian.com/global-development-professionals-network/2015/jun/22/ ethiopia-higher-eduction-universities-development.

8. Damtew Teferra, "Private Higher Education in Ethiopia," *International Higher Education* 40 (May 2005): https://doi.org/10.6017/ihe.2005.40.7495.

9. Tom Bundervoet, Habtamu Neda Fuje, Marco Ranzani, Simon Lange, Atsushi Limi, and Eyasu Tsehaye, *Ethiopia - Employment and Jobs Study (English)* (Washington, DC: World Bank Group, 2019), https://documents.worldbank. org/en/publication/documents-reports/ documentdetail/443391562238337443/ethiopia-employment-and-jobs-study.

10. "Ethiopia: Unemployment Rate from 2004 to 2023," Statista, accessed September 24, 2024, https://www. statista.com/statistics/808436/unemployment-rate-in-ethiopia/.

11. Tebeje Molla and Dawit Tibebu Tiruneh, "Ethiopia's Education System is in Crisis—Now's the Time to Fix It," The Conversation, November 23, 2023, https:// theconversation.com/ethiopias-education-system-is-in-crisis-nows-the-time-to-fix-it-217817.

Chapter Eight

1. Yuval Noah Harari, *Sapiens: A Brief History of Humankind* (Harper Perennial, 2018).

2. "Labor Productivity in Ethiopia Grows 4.9% Annually," Capital Ethiopia, February 24, 2020, https://www.capitalethiopia.com/2020/02/24/labor-productivity-in-ethiopia-grows-4-9-annually/.

3. "Ethiopia Productivity Report," PowerPoint presentation, Launch Workshop, Intercontinental Hotel in Addis Ababa, February 17, 2020, https://gdforum.sakura.ne.jp/en/af-growth/support_ethiopia/document/2020.02_ET/200217Reportlaunchworkshop_final.pdf.

4. Ashenafi Endale, "Ethiopia's Vicious Cycle of Infeasible Loans, Unrealistic Public Projects," *The Reporter*, December 31, 2022, https://www.thereporterethiopia.com/29247/.

5. Kenneth Blanchard and Spencer Johnson, *The One Minute Manager* (Simon & Schuster, 2001).

6. John Doerr, *Measure What Matters: How Google, Bono, and the Gates Foundation Rock the World with OKRs* (Portfolio, 2018).

7. Sarah Harvey, *Kaizen: The Japanese Method for Transforming Habits, One Small Step at a Time* (Pan Macmillan UK, 2019).

8. Jocko Willink and Leif Babin, *Extreme Ownership: How U.S. Navy Seals Lead and Win* (St. Martin's Press, 2015).

9. Angela Duckworth, *Grit: The Power of Passion and Perseverance* (Scribner, 2016).

1. "All the Latest Developments in the Philippine Call Center Industry in 2023," *Superstaff Outsourcing* (blog), March 1, 2023, https://www.superstaff.com/blog/philippine-call-center-industry/.

2. "How Outsourcing is Shaping the Philippines Economy and Society," *CSV Now* (blog), accessed September 24, 2024, https://csvnow.com/blog/effects-of-outsourcing-in-the-philippines.

3. "Why Businesses Hire Indian Companies for Software Development?," *Nasscom Community* (blog), November 11, 2021, https://community.nasscom.in/communities/productstartups/why-businesses-hire-indian-companies-software-development.

4. "The Top 10 Largest Economies in the World in 2024," *Forbes India*, August 19, 2024, https://www.forbesindia.com/article/explainers/top-10-largest-economies-in-the-world/86159/1.

5. "IT Outsourcing - India," Statista, updated April 2024, https://www.statista.com/outlook/tmo/it-services/it-outsourcing/india.

6. Dawit Endeshaw, "Ethiopia's Birr Drops 30% as Central Bank Floats Currency," Reuters, July 29, 2024, https://www.reuters.com/markets/currencies/ethiopia-shifts-market-based-foreign-exchange-system-2024-07-29/.

7. Fred Harter, "How Ethiopia's Currency Float and IMF Deal Are Empowering Economic Reform," The Africa Report, August 21, 2024, https://www.theafricareport.com/359048/how-ethiopias-currency-float-and-imf-deal-are-powering-economic-reform/.

8. "BPO Industry Lobbies for Support to Establish Ethiopia as an Outsourcing Hub," Nanyang Technological University, July 26, 2023, https://www.ntu.edu.sg/cas/news-events/news/details/bpo-industry-lobbies-for-support-to-establish-ethiopia-as-an-outsourcing-hub.

9. "Ethiopian Time," Embassy of Ethiopia, accessed September 24, 2024, https://ethiopianembassy.org/ethiopian-time/.

10. "Digital Hiccup," Ethiopian Business Review, June 11, 2023, https://ethiopianbusinessreview.net/digital-hiccup/.

11. "'No Timeline' for Restoring Internet to Tigray: Ethiopia Minister," Aljazeera, November 30, 2022, https://www.aljazeera.com/news/2022/11/30/no-timeline-for-restoring-internet-to-tigray-ethiopia-minister.

12. "Can Africa's New Free Trade Treaty Boost Business on the Continent?" Al Jazeera, February 16, 2024, https://www.aljazeera.com/news/2024/2/16/afcfta-can-africas-new-trade-treaty-boost-business-on-the-continent.

13. "AFCFTA Supporting the African Continental Free Trade Arena," United Nations Development Programme Africa, accessed September 24, 2024, https://www.undp.org/africa/afcfta-supporting-african-continental-free-trade-area.

14. "The African Continental Free Trade Area," World Bank Group, July 27, 2020, https://www.worldbank.org/en/topic/trade/publication/the-african-continental-free-trade-area.

15. "Ethiopia," OEC, accessed September 24, 2024, https://oec.world/en/profile/country/eth.

16. Samuel Bogale, "Investment Board Lays Groundwork for Trade Business Liberalization," *The Reporter*, April 14, 2024, https://www.thereporterethiopia.com/39646/#google_vignette.

17. "Desire of Foreign Companies to Invest in Ethiopia Growing: Ethiopian Ambassadors," Ethiopian News Agency, January 28, 2024, https://www.ena.et/web/eng/w/eng_3932920.

18. Michael Tesfaye Hiruy, "Ethiopia's Digital Dawn: The Launch of the Digital Transformation Council," Andalem, accessed September 24, 2024, https://andalem.com/ethiopias-digital-dawn-the-launch-of-the-digital-transformation-council/.

ABOUT THE
AUTHOR

Meried Bekele is an entrepreneur, network architect, and speaker. His company, IE Networks, is Ethiopia's leading IT solutions provider, with specializations in enterprise network services, business AI, smart infrastructure, cloud services, and end-to-end IT services. Founded in 2008, IE Networks now has over 200 certified employees and has collaborated with major global brands and notable Ethiopian services. Although IE Networks places technology and innovation at the center of all change, its mission statement reflects larger ambitions: to change the life of Africa through a disciplined work culture and systems thinking.

The diligence and high aspirations of IE Networks mimic that of its CEO. Meried began his career as a network engineer in the data centers of private and federal companies. Working anywhere from 80 to 100 hours per week, he quickly earned a reputation as a hard worker and fast learner. Because of this persistence, at the age of 24, Meried was able to leave Ethiopia for the first time to obtain a CCIE certification, a prestigious credential that is often likened to a PhD in the networking field. On his first attempt, Meried passed the exam and became the only CCIE in Ethiopia.

Meried earned his bachelor's degree in electrical engineering from Mekelle University and his MBA in IT management from Trident University International. He also attended several courses as part of the Harvard Business

School and the Stanford Transformation Program. In the future, Meried looks forward to expanding IE Networks, encouraging an open market, supporting legislative change, inviting international investors, and facilitating a brighter future for Ethiopian entrepreneurs.

www.ingramcontent.com/pod-product-compliance
Lightning Source LLC
Chambersburg PA
CBHW071225210326
41597CB00016B/1945